Mountain Biking on the
North Downs

About the Author

Peter Edwards grew up in Sussex and nurtured a love of walking and mountain biking amid the 'blunt, bow-headed, whale-backed' hills of the South Downs. He has undertaken numerous walking and cycling expeditions in Europe and beyond and is particularly drawn to wild and remote landscapes. Peter completed his doctorate at Sussex University in 2005 and moved to Scotland in 2006. He currently lives in Glasgow with his wife, Fiona, and Dougal the Labrador. Peter also writes about his walking and cycling trips on his blog site at www.writesofway.com.

Other Cicerone guides by the author

Mountain Biking on the South Downs
Walking on Jura, Islay and Colonsay
Walking on Rum and the Small Isles

Mountain Biking on the
North Downs

by Peter Edwards

Emergencies

Always carry a charged mobile phone with you so that emergency services can be alerted in case of serious injury.

If you do need to report such an injury, first make a note of all relevant details including location (with grid reference if possible), the nature of the injury and your mobile phone number. Then call 999 and ask for both Police and Ambulance.

Be ready to give the location and nature of the incident and the numbers of any phones carried by the party. Do not change your position until you are contacted by the emergency services.

There are Accident and Emergency departments at the following hospitals: The Royal Surrey County, Guildford; Dorking General; East Surrey, Redhill; Maidstone; Sevenoaks; St Peter's, Ashford; The Buckland, Dover.

For more information on emergencies and mountain biking safety, see 'Safety' in the introduction.

OS MAP SYMBOLS

main route/stage number

start point/finish point

start/finish point

direction of main route

variant route/stage number

alternative start point/finish point

alternative start/finish point

alternative start/finish stage

direction of variant/alternative route

pub, café, shop

For full OS symbols key see OS maps.

DIFFICULTY GRADES

■ medium

▲ hard

◆ very hard

PROFILE SYMBOLS

train station

P car park

✗ path crossing/junction

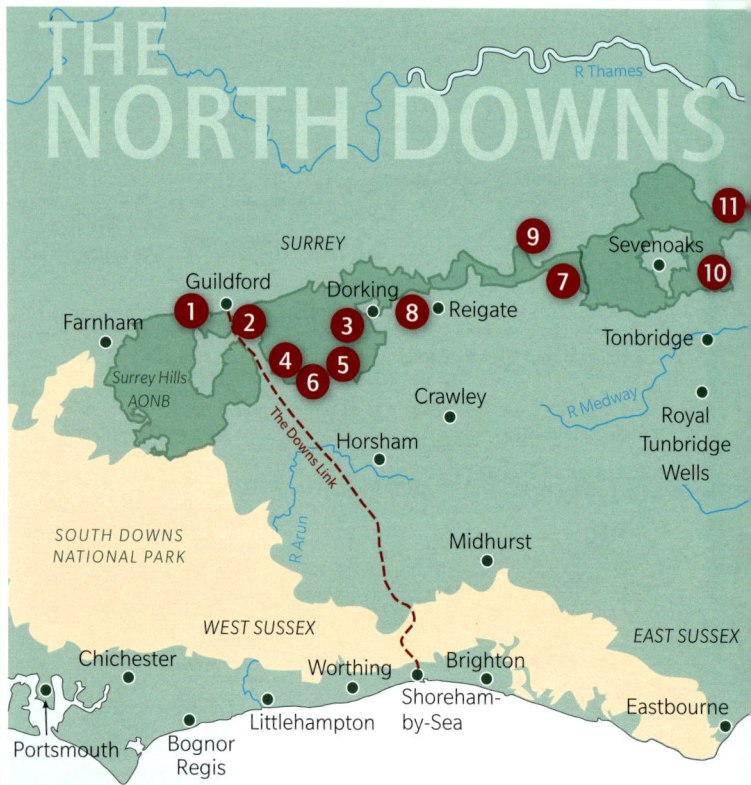

THE NORTH DOWNS

KEY

ROUTES AROUND GUILDFORD

Route 1 ■ Puttenham Common loop
Route 2 ▲ St Martha's Hill–Abinger loop

ROUTES AROUND DORKING

Route 3 ▲ Hackhurst Downs–Polesden Lacey loop
Route 4 ▲ Gomshall–Westhumble loop
Route 5 ▲ Leith Hill and Holmbury Hill loop
Route 6 ◆ Surrey Hills Grand Traverse

ROUTES AROUND REIGATE AND REDHILL

Route 7 ▲ Oxted and Bletchingley loop
Route 8 ▲ Box Hill–Banstead Heath loop
Route 9 ▲ Warlingham–Biggin Hill loop

ROUTES AROUND MAIDSTONE AND THE MEDWAY VALLEY

Route 10 ▲ Oldbury Hill and Mereworth Woods
Route 11 ▲ Meopham–Wrotham loop
Route 12 ▲ Bearsted, Detling Hill and Blue Bell Hill

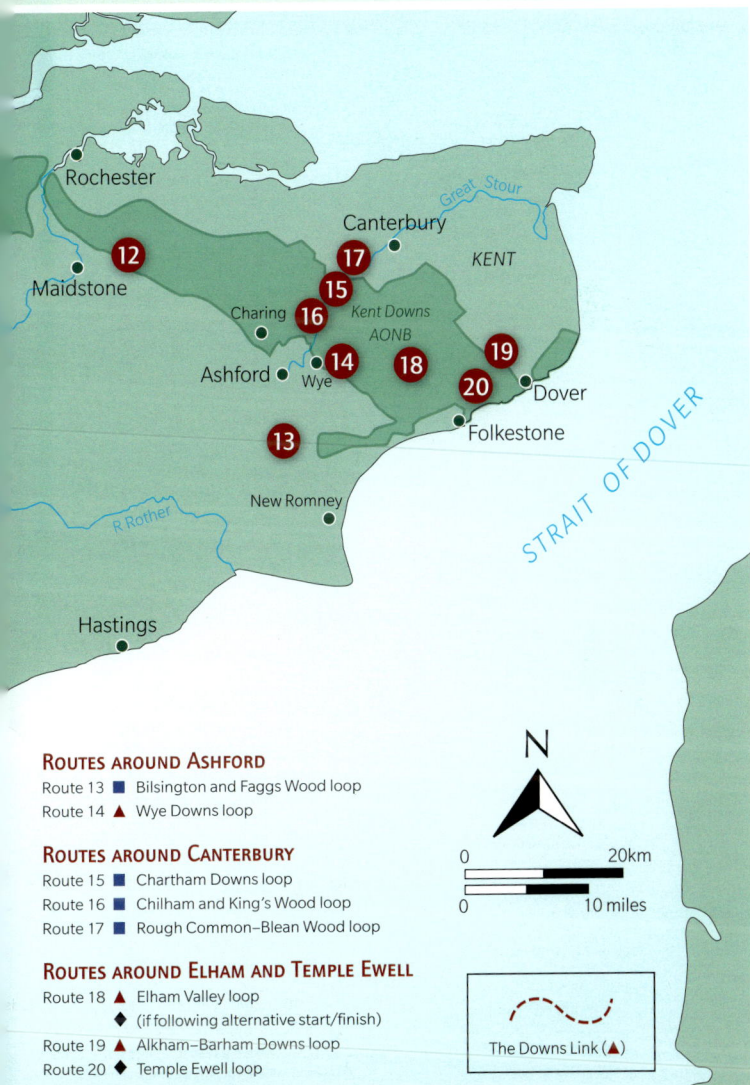

ROUTES AROUND ASHFORD

Route 13 ■ Bilsington and Faggs Wood loop
Route 14 ▲ Wye Downs loop

ROUTES AROUND CANTERBURY

Route 15 ■ Chartham Downs loop
Route 16 ■ Chilham and King's Wood loop
Route 17 ■ Rough Common–Blean Wood loop

ROUTES AROUND ELHAM AND TEMPLE EWELL

Route 18 ▲ Elham Valley loop
       ◆ (if following alternative start/finish)
Route 19 ▲ Alkham–Barham Downs loop
Route 20 ◆ Temple Ewell loop

The Downs Link (▲)

Route	Title	Start/Finish
1	Puttenham Common loop	Puttenham Common car park SU 921 461; or Guildford train station SU 992 496
2	St Martha's Hill–Abinger loop	Guildford train station SU 992 496; or Echo Pit Road car park TQ 004 484
3	Hackhurst Downs–Polesden Lacey loop	Dorking train station TQ 171 504; or Abinger Roughs car park TQ 110 480
4	Gomshall–Westhumble loop	Gomshall train station TQ 089 478; or Dorking train station TQ 171 504
5	Leith Hill–Holmbury Hill loop	Dorking train station TQ 171 504; or Abinger Roughs car park TQ 110 480
6	Surrey Hills Grand Traverse	Abinger Roughs car park TQ 110 480; or Dorking train station TQ 171 504
7	Oxted and Bletchingley loop	Oxted train station TQ 393 529
8	Box Hill–Banstead Heath loop	Reigate train station TQ 254 507
9	Warlingham–Biggin Hill loop	Purley train station TQ 315 615
10	Oldbury Hill and Mereworth Woods	Borough Green train station TQ 609 574; or Oldbury Lane TQ 587 565
11	Meopham–Wrotham loop	Meopham train station TQ 641 679; or Meopham Green TQ 641 651
12	Bearsted, Detling Hill and Blue Bell Hill	Bearstead station TQ 799 561; or Hucking car park TQ 848 581
13	Bilsington and Faggs Wood loop	Hamstreet train station TR 001 337
14	Wye Downs loop	Wye train station TR 048 470
15	Chartham Downs loop	Larkey Valley car park TR 124 557; or Chartham train station TR 107 552
16	Chilham and King's Wood loop	Car park in Chilham TR 067 536; or Chilham train station TR 078 537
17	Rough Common–Blean Wood loop	Canterbury West train station TR 145 584; or car park at Rough Common TR 122 594
18	Elham Valley loop	Elham TR 177 439; or Sandling train station TR 148 368
19	Alkham–Barham Downs loop	Kearsney train station TR 289 440; or Kearsney Abbey car park TR 289 438
20	Temple Ewell loop	Kearsney train station TR 289 440; or Kearsney Abbey car park TR 289 438
	The Downs Link	Start: Trailhead at St Martha's Hill TQ 032 484; or Guildford train station SU 992 496. Finish: Shoreham-by-Sea TQ 218 053; or Brighton train station TQ 310 049

Distance	% off road	Ascent	Grade	Time
18.5km (11½ miles); or 25.75km (16 miles)	80%	370m (1215ft); or 560m (1835ft)	■	2hrs 30mins–3hrs; or 3hrs–3hrs 30mins
28.5km (17¾ miles)	75%	550m (1805ft)	▲	4hrs–4hrs 30mins
27.5km (17 miles); or 22.5km (14 miles)	75%	555m (1820ft); or 480m (1575ft)	▲	2hrs 30mins–3hrs; or 2hrs–2hrs 30mins
29.75km (18½ miles); or 32.25km (20 miles)	80%	635m (2080ft); or 710m (2330ft)	▲	3hrs–3hrs 30mins; or 3hrs 15mins–3hrs 45mins
33.5km (20¾ miles); or 22.5km (14 miles)	65%	745m (2445ft); or 550m (1805ft)	▲	3hrs–3hrs 30mins; or 2hrs 30mins–3hrs
41.5km (25¾ miles); or 54km (33½ miles)	85%	1010m (3315ft); or 1205m (3955ft)	◆	4hrs–4hrs 30mins; or 5hrs 30mins–6hrs
24km (15 miles)	60%	615m (2020ft)	■	3hrs–3hrs 30mins
29.75km (18½ miles)	80%	635m (2085ft)	▲	3hrs 30mins–4hrs
38km (23½ miles)	55%	795m (2610ft)	▲	3hrs 30mins–4hrs
27.5km (17 miles)	65%	550m (1805ft)	▲	4hrs 30mins–5hrs
38.75km (24 miles)	60%	755m (2475ft)	▲	4hrs 30mins–5hrs
47.5km (29 miles); or 33.5km (21 miles)	55%	925m (3035ft); or 620m (2035ft)	▲	4hrs 30mins–5hrs 30mins; or 3hrs–4hrs
25.75km (16 miles)	60%	200m (655ft)	■	2hrs 30mins–3hrs 30mins
21.5km (13¾ miles)	70%	510m (1675ft)	▲	2hrs 30mins–3hrs
20km (12½ miles)	60%	305m (1000ft)	■	2hrs 30mins–3hrs
22km (13¾ miles)	60%	350m (1150ft)	■	2hrs 30mins–3hrs
31.5km (19½ miles); or 29.75km (18½ miles)	60%	440m (1445ft); or 410m (1345ft)	■	3hrs–3hrs 30mins
23km (14 miles); or 41.75km (26 miles)	50%	445m (1460ft); or 830m (2725ft)	▲; or ◆	3hrs–3hrs 30mins; or 5hrs 30mins–6hrs 30mins
40.5km (25 miles)	55%	745m (2445ft)	▲	3hrs–4hrs
34.75km (21¾ miles)	60%	585m (1920ft)	◆	3hrs 30mins–4hrs
59km (37 miles); or 77.5km (48¼ miles)	90%	465m (1525ft); or 705m (2315ft)	▲	4hrs–4hrs 30mins; or 5hrs 30mins–6hrs

Hanging on in the Surrey Hills – a fast descent near Holmbury Hill (Route 6; photo: Jen Dodd)

Introduction

For the enthusiastic mountain biker the North Downs is nirvana in the Home Counties! Some of the finest off-road trails to be found anywhere in the country are available in abundance amid the green, rolling chalk and sandstone hills and along the steep, wooded escarpments that comprise some of England's loveliest countryside. The North Downs are criss-crossed by hundreds of kilometres of well-maintained byways and bridleways that are accessible to mountain bikers and which can be mixed and matched into almost infinitely variable route combinations. The adventurous mountain biker will not be short of options in this corner of the country.

Mountain bikers are attracted to the area in their droves from the southeast of England and beyond. Partly this is because of its proximity to London, but mostly it is due to the riding terrain. From chalk and flint bridleways to loose sand tracks and sinuous forest singletrack; rough, tough climbs to seemingly endless rattling descents; the dry and dusty to the wet and muddy, the North Downs are packed with variety.

The narrow spine of the Hog's Back between Farnham and Guildford forms the western extremity of the North Downs, which encompasses the ancient chalk downlands, heathlands, pasture and woodlands of Surrey and Kent, while the iconic cliffs of the English Channel coast between Folkestone and Deal terminate the ridge in the east. The south-facing escarpment of the North Downs is generally very steep while a dip slope descends more gradually to the north. The greatest concentration of quality mountain biking trails is at the western end of the Downs among the Surrey Hills – a true mountain biker's paradise because of the sheer number and variety of excellent trails, both natural and man-made. The many fine byways, bridleways and country lanes of southeast Kent are less well-known as a mountain biking destination, but are in fact something of a hidden gem – partly because so many riders are drawn to the glamorous trails of the Surrey Hills and the South Downs.

As well as the extensive network of well-maintained byways and

Lift off! Big air on the Surrey Hills (Routes 5 and 6)

Trail (NDW). The Greensand Way (GW) is another long-distance path that traverses part of the North Downs area; much of it is also comprised of bridleways and byways, hence it also makes regular appearances in this guidebook. Many of these rights of way – including sections of the NDW – are accessible to and very popular with horse riders and mountain bikers as well as walkers.

ABOUT THE ROUTES IN THIS GUIDE

The routes in this guidebook are day, half-day and shorter routes distributed along the length and breadth of the Downs. Routes 1 to 9 are located in or on the periphery of the Surrey Hills AONB and Routes 10 to 20 are located in or on the periphery of the Kent Downs AONB. The routes are divided into area sections in the guide. The area sections are roughly analogous with the areas covered by the various Ordnance Survey Explorer maps covering the North Downs (see 'Maps'; p25). As mentioned above, there is a greater concentration of routes in the Surrey Hills and in southeast Kent as many of the best trails are to be found in these areas. Good quality bridleways and byways are a bit thin of the ground in east Surrey and west Kent.

There is no description of a complete traverse of the NDW included here for the principal reason that much of the NDW is footpath-only, hence off-limits to mountain bikers. Alternative routes are too dependent

bridleways criss-crossing the North Downs, there are also many purpose-built mountain bike trails in the Surrey Hills area in particular. Many of the tracks and trails traverse chalk and sandstone downland, which is generally well-drained and provides superlative mountain biking conditions for much of the year. However, the North Downs is also a diverse landscape comprising a variety of terrain, including woodland, pasture and heathland. These ancient downlands comprise two Areas of Outstanding Natural Beauty (AONBs) – the Surrey Hills and Kent Downs – some of Britain's most iconic and best-loved landscapes.

The North Downs contains many hundreds of kilometres of public rights of way, including the 246km (153-mile) North Downs Way National

on roads to make the traverse of the NDW by mountain bike a particularly enjoyable prospect.

This guidebook does not include routes for trail centres near the North Downs, such as Bedgebury and PORC (Penshurst Off Road Club) in Kent; the main reason being that route descriptions are superfluous for what are essentially turn up and ride trails, way-marked in some cases and self-evident in others. These dedicated trails are well worth visiting, especially for those with a fondness for singletrack and downhilling trails.

The route descriptions pay special attention to the nature of the terrain encountered as well as the major climbs and descents involved and any particular hazards of which to be aware. Facilities and services en route are also included. The routes are designed for maximum enjoyment of the mountain biking potential available on the North Downs, so there is some overlap and repetition in the use of particular stretches of bridleway and byway between several of the routes. Roads are avoided wherever practical, although in many cases stretches of road (mostly quiet country lanes) here and there can link up some great off-road trails.

CENTRES

The routes in this guidebook are distributed along the length and breadth of the North Downs. Centres include: Guildford, Dorking, Peaslake, Reigate, Oxted, Bearsted, Chilham, Chartham, Wye, Wrotham, Meopham, Elham and Temple Ewell.

GETTING THERE AND GETTING AROUND

Essentially, there are two options for getting to the North Downs. Firstly, the area is well-served by the rail network. All the main centres along the North Downs are served by mainline routes from London and other areas of south-east England. There are also good rail links between London and the main towns around the North Downs and the branch-line stations in-between. All of the rides in this guide can be started from, and finished at, nearby railway stations and there are also options for extending or cutting short rides by means of other railway stations near most of the routes.

Most trains serving the North Downs area have dedicated space for two bikes, which is barely adequate. Although they can go in the door areas, it can be a hassle if you have to keep moving yours to let people off and on. Engineering works sometimes take place at the weekend on the southern rail network, and rail replacement buses do not carry bikes – so check before travelling. There are rush hour restrictions on taking bikes into and out of London on most lines in southeast England, so check these out before making your journey. Timetable information, as well as information on engineering works and on bike restrictions, can be found at www.nationalrail.co.uk or tel 08457 484950.

The second option is to travel by car. There are car parks at many sites all the way along the North Downs, which can make travelling by car more convenient (car parks are indicated on the route maps) than by train because of time restrictions, engineering works and long-winded rail connections. However, the less traffic there is around the Downs the better for everyone, so please leave your car at home if you can.

WHEN TO GO

The North Downs are superb for mountain biking all year round and each season has its own particular charms. Obviously downland bridleways and byways are at their driest in summer – when you can fairly zip along the ridges and enjoy greater traction on the uphills. The summer months are also much busier than other seasons, especially at weekends and during the school summer

holidays, requiring mountain bikers to be more aware of walkers, horse riders and other people out enjoying the Downs.

Spring and autumn are that bit quieter, but the weather and therefore conditions on the ground are obviously less predictable. Winter can be an excellent time for mountain biking on the Downs, so long as you're not frightened of getting a bit (or a lot) muddy. However, after prolonged periods of rain the ground can be transformed into a highly adhesive quagmire in places, completely clogging-up your bike and actually rendering riding impossible. Wet sand can also be detrimental to your bike. See 'Tools and maintenance' (p20) on how to avoid damage. This is no excuse to avoid the Downs in winter as there are plenty of well-drained areas where mud and wet sand are not so much of a problem. Areas that are particularly prone to mud are indicated in the route descriptions.

SAFETY

Most of the time, mountain biking is a perfectly safe activity and far safer than cycling on roads. Rutted, slippery and loose surfaces are frequently encountered, however, and if you take a tumble at speed, you risk causing yourself considerable damage. Riding downhill at speed is one of the great joys of mountain biking, but it is essential that you maintain control. If you can't see what (or who) is coming round a bend, slow down.

Much of the North Downs is well served by railway links

Catching a breather in picturesque Peaslake before tackling Holmbury Hill (Route 6)

Likewise, if you have never ridden a particular downhill before and do not know what to anticipate, moderate your speed.

Make sure that your brakes are working efficiently and that your tyres are inflated properly (30–40psi, depending on terrain, conditions, your weight and so on), under-inflated tyres are more vulnerable to 'pinch' punctures or 'snake bites' – where the inner tube is pinched between the rim and a rock, kerb or rut, for example. Check that all quick release levers are tight and wheels are secure.

It is recommended that you always wear a helmet and appropriate clothing, and carry a first aid kit, plenty of water, some high-energy snacks, a map and compass (or GPS) as well as a mobile phone, and wear sun block in summer. Carry waterproofs in wet weather. Carry spare inner tubes, a puncture repair kit, a pump and basic tool kit. Carry lights if there is any chance that you will be returning during or after dusk.

If you go riding on your own, let someone know where you are going and when you expect to return. In the event of a serious accident requiring urgent assistance, dial 999 and ask for both the police and ambulance. Be ready to give a map grid reference.

Equipment

Your bike

Out on the bridleways and byways of the North Downs you will encounter mountain bikers riding machines costing between a few hundred pounds

Pedal and Spoke, bike hire/shop in Peaslake (Route 5)

and a few thousand. Your choice of bike is contingent on a number of factors, but is generally the sum of disposable income divided by degree of enthusiasm. There is no doubt that a top of the range, lightweight bike with high-specification components can only add to the enjoyment of off-road riding. However, there is little point spending thousands on a bike that only sees action a few times a year; for those who are serious about their sport, a good quality machine is essential. A far more important business than the relative cost of the bike is choosing the right type of mountain bike for you – it is best to seek advice from reputable bike retailers before buying.

Choosing the right frame size is a crucial factor, bearing in mind that a smaller frame than you would need for a road bike is better suited for off-road riding. An increasing number of mountain bikers ride full-suspension bikes, which take the edge off the bone-jarring sensations experienced on rougher terrain; a smoother ride also means greater control, especially on downhills and 'technical' terrain. Many of the trails encountered on the North Downs are as appropriate terrain for full-suspension bikes as anywhere, although many people still prefer to ride 'hardtail' machines – that is, front suspension only – which are lighter and faster uphill. This is a matter of personal preference dictated in part by the kind of riding you do.

Helmet

The vast majority of mountain bikers wear a helmet, with very good reason. The nature of the activity means that taking a tumble is a likelihood at some point. If this happens when you are travelling downhill at speed you are at risk of serious harm. As well as injuries such as broken bones and serious gashes, a blow to the head can be fatal or cause permanent disability or paralysis. A helmet may not prevent such serious injuries in some cases, but in others it might.

Full face helmet and body armour on Holmbury Hill – a sensible choice for downhilling enthusiasts (Route 6)

Body armour

Some areas of the North Downs – the Surrey Hills in particular – are popular venues for downhilling and free riding, highly technical riding that involves negotiating jumps and various obstacles – both natural and those made by 'trail builders' – preferably at high speed. Unsurprisingly, enthusiasts often wear full-face helmets, neck braces and body armour, again, with good reason.

Body armour is cumbersome and unnecessary for the less death-defying activity of cross country (or XC, as some style it) mountain biking, but if you like to take on a few jumps here and there, then shin, knee and elbow pads should be considered.

First aid kit

Anecdotal evidence suggests that a majority of mountain bikers do not carry a first aid kit with them. Granted that a first aid kit is not much use if you break a collarbone – a not uncommon injury among mountain bikers, but there are plenty of occasions where a dressing, antiseptic wipes and painkillers can be very useful. Downland chalk is full of hard and sharp flints that can cause nasty gashes. All the more reason to wear a helmet.

Eyewear

Many riders wear sunglasses to reduce glare on bright days, but also as protection from mud, debris and flying insects – especially on fast descents. There are many

All kitted out in Gorsehill Wood (Route 20)

bike-specific sunglasses on the market, some of which have interchangeable lenses with different colours for different light conditions. Downhillers and free riders sometimes wear ski goggles.

Clothing

There is no shortage of biking-specific clothing on the market and specialised off-road gear comprises a significant part of this. With the funds and inclination, many hundreds of pounds can be spent on equipping yourself for off-road riding and for dedicated enthusiasts it may constitute money well spent. However, there are some essentials worth considering even for infrequent mountain bikers. Wickable base layers, underwear, mid-layers and top layers can make what is often a sweaty activity much more comfortable. Stopping for a breather in a sweat-drenched cotton top is asking for trouble even in a light breeze. Shorts or wickable undershorts with a padded seat ensure a more comfortable relationship with your saddle, especially on longer rides.

Biking-specific waterproofs are designed for a close fit and freedom of movement so as to avoid drag or getting caught up in your bike's moving parts. Waterproofs should be a 'breathable' material, such as Gore-Tex.

Many mountain bikers use the Shimano Pedalling Dynamics (SPD) system with shoes that clip onto the pedal using cleats, which provides greater stability and makes pedalling more efficient by engaging the 'backstroke'. Whether using SPDs, 'platform' pedals or other systems, waterproof overshoes or waterproof socks can be useful in wet conditions.

Gloves improve grip on your handlebars, keep your hands warm in winter and provide protection when you fall off.

TOOLS AND MAINTENANCE

Whatever choices you make about the type of bike you ride, the more use it gets the more maintenance it will require. However expensive or inexpensive your bike, it needs to be looked after. Off-road riding can take it out of a bike, especially in wet and muddy conditions. It is important to keep your bike at least reasonably clean and keep its moving parts lubricated. A well-maintained bike performs better and its components will last longer.

In dry periods during the summer months, many paths on the North Downs develop a thick layer of fine chalk or earth dust; loose, dry sand is also a feature in some areas. Combined with ordinary chain oil, dust and sand produce a highly effective grinding paste that will punish your bike's drive-train. Wet sand (a problem after substantial rainfall) has the same effect. Using a 'dry' teflon chain lubricant reduces this phenomenon.

Learning the basics of bike maintenance and equipping yourself with elementary tools is a good idea. You should carry a small tool-kit and pump with you while out riding and, at the very least, be able to repair a puncture, fix a broken chain and adjust your brakes and gears when necessary. A basic tool-kit including a puncture repair kit, spare inner tubes, tyre levers, allen key set, spoke key and chain link extractor can be carried in a saddlepack or backpack.

NAVIGATION

Many walkers and cyclists now use GPS (global positioning system) for navigation: a number of biking-specific GPS are now on the market. A GPS can make navigation easy and accurate and dispense with the need to carry maps. On the down side, they are not cheap and they are not infallible. For those without a GPS, a map and compass are just as useful

Holmbury Hill, one of the many wooded hills in Surrey and Kent, where good navigation is all the more important (Routes 5 and 6)

for mountain bikers in unfamiliar territory as they are for walkers, although very few of the former seem to carry compasses. Although waymarking on the North Downs is extensive, it is still possible to lose your way – especially in wooded areas, and a compass can help prevent you heading miles off course.

Fuel stop in Peaslake, Surrey Hills (Route 6)

HYDRATION

Always make sure you have plenty of water with you especially during the summer and on longer rides. Many mountain bikers use hydration packs – a water reservoir with a drinking tube, usually with two or three litres' capacity, carried in a purpose-designed, small backpack. Hydration packs allow you to carry more water than water bottles carried in frame-mounted bottle cages – which are more popular with road cyclists – that can easily be dislodged when riding off-road. Be sure to be adequately hydrated before setting off on your ride.

MTB-specific backpacks, which are designed to carry water reservoirs, come in various capacities and are usually designed to carry the essentials (tools, pump, waterproofs, snacks, mobile phone, first aid kit, map) in internal pockets. They are also designed for a comfortable and stable fit for riding. If you are thinking about acquiring one, consider how much capacity you will need for the kind of riding you do.

FOOD

Carry enough food and/or make certain you can buy some food en route. If your energy levels dip when riding it is difficult to maintain output on an empty tank. When walking, hunger can be ignored to a certain extent, but mountain bikers and road cyclists are prey to the phenomenon of gnawing pangs that will not go away, which is known in some parts as 'bonking'. It makes sense to carry lightweight, high-energy foods such as flapjacks, trail mix, 'hi-energy' bars and bananas – although try not to take a tumble if carrying the latter.

RIGHTS OF WAY AND OTHER USERS

Mountain bikers have 'right of way' on bridleways, permissive bridleways, byways, green lanes and some white roads. This gives you the right to share the way with other users; nonetheless, you should always give way to walkers and horse riders. Do not

The Bikers' Code

- Don't ride on footpaths. It's illegal, it can damage paths and sensitive heathland environments, and it's really annoying for walkers. Furthermore, the bridleway and byway network on the North Downs is so extensive that there really is no need to use footpaths.

- Only ride at speeds that are safe for the trail ahead. You don't know what's around the next corner.

- Make other users aware of your presence by calling out a greeting if approaching walkers or horse riders from the rear.

- Always give way to horse riders and walkers.

- Be respectful and courteous to other users.

- Choose your route carefully, especially when the ground is wet, to minimise erosion.

- Avoid abrupt braking and skidding, thus reducing trail damage.

- Make sure your bike is safe to ride and be prepared for emergencies.

- Wear a helmet and protective clothing.

approach walkers or horse riders at speed from behind or in front. When approaching from behind, slow right down and announce your presence with a 'hello' so as not to startle man or beast. When approaching from the front, slow down and give a wide berth or stop and make way for them to pass you (some riders use a bell, but experience suggests that some walkers and horse riders find bell-tinkling mountain bikers irksome in the extreme!).

This is more than a matter of politeness; if you approach walkers or horse riders at speed and/or fail to warn of your presence then you might cause a serious accident. There are already far too many walkers and horse riders with a low opinion of mountain bikers as it is and poor behaviour may mean certain rights of way being closed to mountain bikers in future. For example, a couple of routes in the Ashdown Forest (a large area of open heathland, just to the south of the North Downs) merited inclusion in this guidebook, however, the Forest is closed to mountain bikers because, several years ago, the Ashdown Forest Conservation Board rejected access for a variety of reasons including concerns about 'biker behaviour' and because of 'considerable opposition from existing Forest users'. In this case the grounds for exclusion are contentious, but the fact remains that we are all ambassadors for our sport and for each other when we are out on the trails.

WAYMARKING

Waymarking on the North Downs is generally excellent, and you will find waymarkers on gates and signposts at regular intervals and at path junctions – where you need them most. Bridleways are indicated with blue arrows and in the case of the NDW those arrows

National Cycle Route signpost

incorporate the acorn emblem, which indicates long-distance paths (LDP) in England and Wales. Byways are indicated with red arrows. Footpaths are indicated with yellow arrows, which are, of course, out of bounds to mountain bikers and horse riders.

Although paths and tracks on the North Downs are usually very well maintained and comprehensively waymarked, it is still quite possible to get lost. Signposts are occasionally removed or damaged, routes can be changed temporarily or permanently for a variety of reasons and it is also quite easy at times to go whizzing past a path junction on your bike, oblivious to any waymarkers. There are also a few places where waymarkers are not obvious or clear; where this has been the case, or there are good chances of going astray for other reasons, then these instances are noted in the route descriptions. Where bridleways and byways were without signage at the time of writing (spring/summer 2013 in most cases) then this is indicated

as: (no signpost/waymarker). Bear in mind that in these cases signposts or waymarkers may have been installed or replaced in the interim.

Another situation where it is easy to get lost is when you are riding

National Cycle Route Millennium Milepost

through managed woodland. Forestry plantations are often criss-crossed with tracks and forestry roads that are liable to change and therefore do not always correspond with the map. It can be quite easy to lose your bearings when all you can see are trees. Hence, carrying a GPS or compass and map can prove extremely useful.

Maps

Ordnance Survey provide map coverage of the North Downs in 1:25,000 and 1:50,000 scales (see www. ordnancesurvey.co.uk/leisure).

The most up to date 1:50,000 scale Ordnance Survey mapping is used for the routes in this guidebook. At the time of going to press, the information on the maps included in this guide was accurate. A note of caution: the status of some rights of way may be changed over time. Most often – although not always – cyclists have been granted greater access rights with footpaths and other rights of way being 'upgraded' to permissive bridleways. Older copies of maps may contain information that is at odds with what is included here.

Roughly half of the 250km NDW National Trail is currently off-limits to bikes. However, at the beginning of 2013 the NDW National Trail's Steering Group commissioned a survey to assess which parts of the trail and nearby rights of way that are currently off-limits could be made accessible.

Ordnance Survey 1:25,000 Explorer series

- 137 Ashford, Headcorn, Chilham & Wye
- 138 Dover, Folkestone & Hythe
- 145 Guildford & Farnham
- 146 Dorking, Box Hill and Reigate
- 147 Sevenoaks & Tonbridge
- 148 Maidstone & The Medway Towns
- 149 Sittingbourne & Faversham
- 150 Canterbury & The Isle of Thanet

Ordnance Survey 1:50,000 Landranger series

- 178 Thames Estuary, Rochester & Southend-on-Sea
- 179 Canterbury, East Kent, Dover & Margate
- 186 Aldershot & Guildford, Camberley & Haslemere
- 187 Dorking & Reigate, Crawley & Horsham
- 188 Maidstone & The Weald of Kent
- 189 Ashford & Romney Marsh, Rye & Folkestone

Harvey Maps publish two lightweight, waterproof 1:40,000 single sheet maps showing the whole of the NDW: North Downs Way (East) and North Downs Way (West): www. harveymaps.co.uk.

Digital Ordnance Survey mapping of the region is available from sources including www.memorymap.co.uk and www.anquet.co.uk.

Splash down! Winter mud – not for the faint-hearted (Route 13)

USING THIS GUIDE

Each of the routes included in this guide are graded according to the degree of physical effort they require. The grades are:

■ medium
▲ hard
◆ very hard

The grades reflect the length of the route, the number and severity of climbs and the nature of the terrain traversed. Aside from the dedicated downhill and free riding trails to be found around the Surrey Hills and elsewhere – route descriptions of which are not included in this guide – there is little 'technical' mountain biking to be found on the North Downs; hence there is no 'difficult' grade. The 'hard' and 'very hard' classifications in this guide focus on how strenuous the routes are. There are no 'easy' routes included here and, therefore, there is no 'easy' grade.

Timings

Each route description has an estimated time for how long it should take to get around. These timings are a rough guide and the actual time will vary depending on fitness and experience, time of year, weather conditions, and possible punctures or mechanical problems, as well as 're-fuelling', pub or café stops. Allow yourself extra time, the first time you ride each of the routes in this guidebook.

Distances

Distances are given in kilometres and metres throughout the route descriptions. The total distance given at the beginning of each route is given in kilometres with the equivalent in miles given in brackets. All distances given in metres are linear distances and not height gain unless specifically stated. 'Climb for 200m along the bridleway' means the climb is over a distance of 200m as opposed to: '...ascend 200m as you climb along the bridleway for 500m'.

The total route distances are also broken down into off-road and on-road distances, with the off-road total given as a percentage. These off-road/on-road distances are as accurate as possible, allowing for a few grey areas where there is some uncertainty as to whether a particular section of a route really qualifies as a 'road' or not!

The route descriptions are detailed and map references are given where opportunities for uncertainty with route-finding occur. Once you have ridden the routes a couple of times they will become more familiar and you can spend less time with your nose in this book! Like following recipes from a cookery book, interpreting these routes in your own way and indulging in a spot of improvisation will adapt them to your own taste.

Although the routes in this guide incorporate the most up-to-date Ordnance Survey 1:50,000 mapping available at the time of publication, it is recommended that you also carry the relevant OS map sheets. You may also wish to carry a GPS as a further guide to navigation. Should you get lost or want to find railway stations, pubs, car parks or villages that are off the route, they will allow you to see the wider context.

ABBREVIATIONS AND SYMBOLS USED IN THE ROUTE DESCRIPTIONS

← left
→ right
↑ straight ahead
✗ path crossing/junction
N north
S south
E east
W west
NW etc. northwest etc.
LH and RH left-hand and right-hand

- Specific directions to readers are given as arrow symbols. Where the words **left** and **right** are in bold, they are not specific route directions to readers but as they describe the physical nature of roads, tracks or paths taken, they are still important for navigation. Where they are not in bold they relate to text that is not crucial to navigation – usually roads, tracks or paths that should not be taken. Where 'left-hand' and 'right-hand' are not abbreviated, they also relate, essentially, to incidental text. An example of how this is handled in the book is: '... as the track turns sharply **right** (N). Keep ↑, ignoring two left-hand turns; at Combe Lane, turn → then sharply ←...'

- Easy to miss paths are noted in **bold green**; warnings of steep, dangerous or possibly crowded routes in **bold red**.

- Place names in route descriptions that appear on their maps are noted in **bold**.

- Roads are shown as A281, motorways as M25.

- Grid references are shown as SU 921 461.

- Important signs along the way are noted in *red italics* in route descriptions.

Further abbreviations

LDP – Long-distance path
NCN – National Cycle Network
NDW – North Downs Way
GW – Greensand Way
DL – Downs Link
EVW – Elham Valley Way
SSW – Saxon Shore Way
CWW – Crab & Winkle Way
PW – Pilgrim's Way
AONB – Area of Outstanding Natural Beauty

Routes around Guildford

Sandy path on the Pilgrim's Way at
The Chantries by St Martha's Hill (Route 2)

In the maze of 'jungle' trails on Puttenham Common

Route 1
Puttenham Common loop

START/FINISH	Puttenham Common car park SU 921 461; or Guildford train station SU 992 496
DISTANCE	18.5km (11½ miles); or 25.75km (16 miles)
ON ROAD	4km (2½ miles); or 7.25km (4½ miles)
OFF ROAD	14.5km (9 miles); or 18.5km (11½ miles)
ASCENT	370m (1215ft); or 560m (1835ft)
GRADE	■
TIME	2hrs 30mins–3hrs; or 3–3hrs 30mins
MAPS	OS Explorer 145 or Landranger 186
PUB	The Good Intent, Puttenham
CAFÉ	The Tea Shop at Watts Gallery, Down Lane near Compton

Overview

This compact route puts together a loop of the best off-road trails available in the area, using bridleways and byways along with narrow country lanes. Excellent sandy tracks are the order of the day, not least on Puttenham Common and along the North Downs Way (NDW). Navigation can be tricky on the wooded sections, so keep your eye on the ball.

There's relatively little climbing involved on the main route, the most significant being a 50-metre climb along the NDW to the north of Puttenham Common. However, the variant route from Guildford involves a steep 100-metre climb out of town to Henley Fort on the

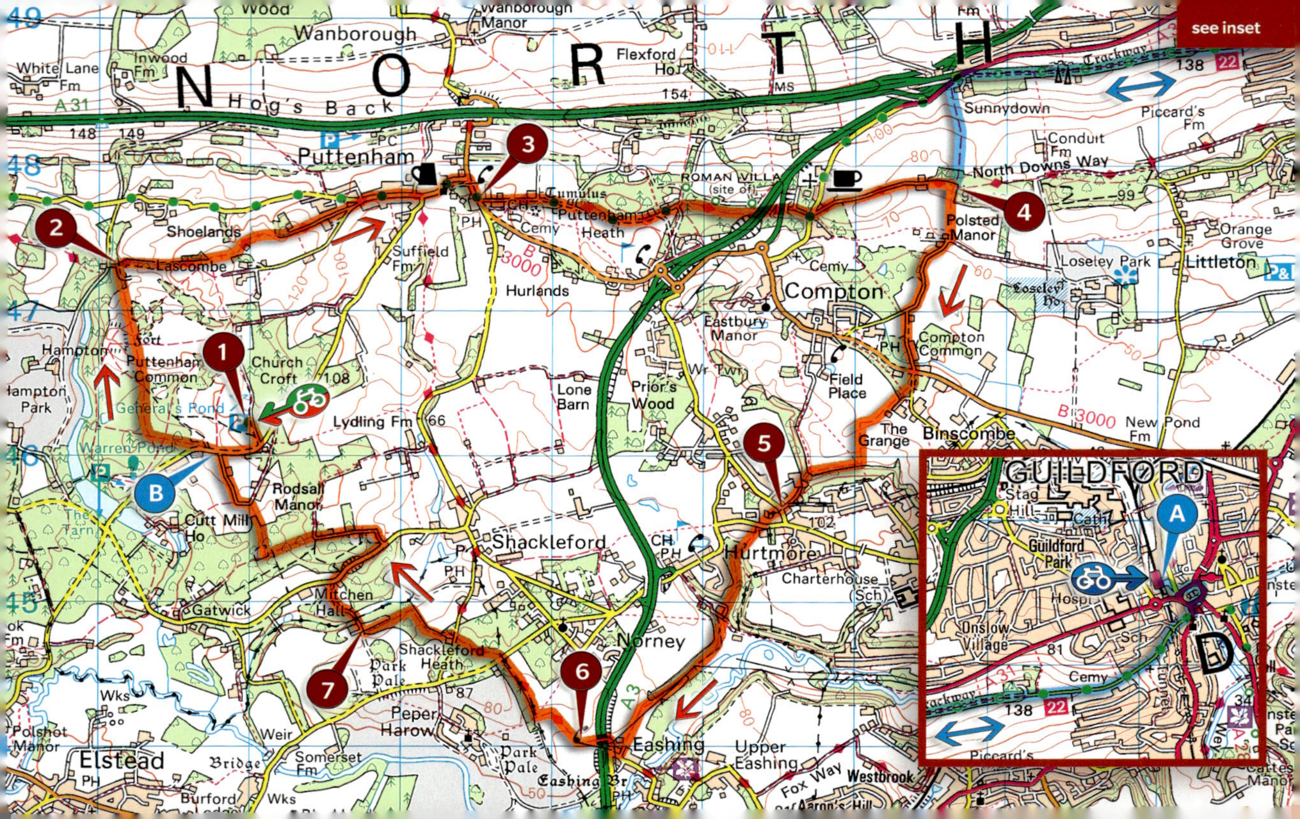

see inset
NORTH
Hog's Back
Wanborough
Wanborough Manor
Flexford Ho
White Lane Fm
Inwood Fm
Puttenham
Shoelands
Lascombe
Suffield Fm
Puttenham Heath
Cemy
Tumulus
Hurlands
ROMAN VILLA (site of)
Sunnydown
Conduit Fm
Piccard's Fm
North Downs Way
Polsted Manor
Orange Grove
Loseley Park
Littleton
Compton
Eastbury Manor
Compton Common
Field Place
Prior's Wood
Lone Barn
Lydling Fm
Church Croft
Hampton
Hampton Park
Puttenham Common
General's Pond
Warren Pond
The Tarn
Rodsall Manor
Cutt Mill Ho
Binscombe
The Grange
New Pond Fm
Shackleford
Hurtmore
Charterhouse (Sch)
Mitchen Hall
Gatwick
Norney
Shackleford Heath
Park Pale
Peper Harow
Eashing
Upper Eashing
Eashing Br
Fox Way
Westbrook
Somerset Fm
Weir
Elstead
Polshot Manor
Burford
Wks
GUILDFORD
Stag Hill
Cath
Guildford Park
Hosp
Onslow Village
Cemy
Tunnel
Trackway
Wey
Piccard's
A31
A3
B3000
1
2
3
4
5
6
7
A
B
D

Hog's Back, but this is mostly on tarmac. On the return, tree roots add an extra dimension to the steep climb up Sunnydown on a narrow path.

Directions

1 Exit the **car park** at the **SE** corner of **Puttenham Common** and turn ➔ onto the road. Take the second signposted bridleway that sits on the **right** after 300m and enter the woods. Follow a narrow sandy path, which is overgrown with bracken ferns in summer, ↑ over a bridleway ✖ then turn ➔ at a second bridleway ✖ (not waymarked). Continue **N** along a sandy track, ignoring turnings to the left and right. Bear ➔ at a bridleway fork at the foot of a rise and climb steeply to a plateau at the top of the common. Continue ↑ (**N**) over a bridleway ✖ then ↑ over a second bridleway ✖ with waymarkers and descend along a narrow sandy path. The path delivers you to a ✖ with a house 100m to the left at Totford Hatch.

2 Turn ➔ along the NDW on a broad sand and stone-metalled byway track and continue steadily uphill. This excellent section of the NDW rises and falls a couple of times before rejoining tarmac at **Lascombe Lane**. At a T-junction with The Street, keep ➔ (↑) and continue through **Puttenham**, passing the **Good Intent** pub and the church before arriving at a T-junction with the B3000. Turn ➔ (with care) and cross straight over the busy road to follow

Heather in blossom on Puttenham Common

a path along the verge for 150m before turning ← onto a broad track road (*North Downs Way*).

3 Continue ↑ to ride initially along the track through a golf links on **Puttenham Heath** then on a sandy path through woodland before emerging at a minor road. Turn → and pass under two road bridges in succession and continue to a T-junction. Turn ← (*Guildford*) then turn → onto a broad sandy track (NDW) by Watts Gallery. Climb a little and arrive at a bridleway ✗ after 1km and turn → off the NDW.

Alternative start from Guildford station

A Follow the one-way system around to join the `B3100` Godalming road. Almost immediately turn → and climb very steeply along The Mount road (*NCN22* (National Cycle Network)). At the top of the climb (Henley Fort) continue ↑ – initially on tarmac then on an earth track – for just over 2km to reach the `A31` just before a major junction. Turn ← along Down Lane then ← again onto a bridleway path after 100m. Descend steeply on the narrow path with

Loose sand along the North Downs Way

tree roots forming natural steps. At the bottom of the descent, climb a little to arrive at a bridleway ✖ and continue ↑ – crossing the NDW.

∙ ∙

4 Descend along a sunken lane that becomes a narrow sandy path (overgrown in summer), which pops out on tarmac by a house. Descend a little along Polsted Lane, bearing ← at a fork and continuing to a T-junction with the **B3000**. Dogleg → then ← along a minor road then soon after turn → onto a signposted bridleway. Continue through woods, keeping → at a fork then turning sharp ← and climbing along a field edge on a narrow path. Turn → to follow the bridleway contouring along the edge of woods before climbing to join a residential road.

5 At the T-junction cross ↑ onto a bridleway between houses. Cross another road to rejoin the bridleway and descend to a path junction. Turn ← and continue descending along a broad sandy track to a T-junction; dogleg → then ← and follow the sandy bridleway track. Go through a gate, continue along a concrete track to a T-Junction and turn →. Before hitting the **A3**, turn → and follow a bridleway over a bridge across the busy road.

6 From the bridge, go through a gate, turn → and follow the path around the field to another gate. Go through and continue ↑ along the bridleway. Cross a road, continue ↑ on the bridleway across **Shackleford Heath**, cross another road and follow the bridleway through woods, bearing ← at a fork and descending a little on a good sandy track.

7 Where the track emerges by a house (Warren Lodge), bear → (no signpost) and continue around to a T-junction with a road. Turn → and climb along the road; at the brow of the hill, turn sharp ← off the road onto a broad byway track. Climb steadily bear ← and continue ↑ on a bridleway where the byway turns sharp right. Turn → at the next bridleway and continue to the road by **Rodsall Manor**. Turn ← along the road and continue around to a T-junction (SU 918 460). Turn → and then ← to return to the **car park**.

Alternative finish at Guildford station

∙ ∙

B Turn ← at the T-junction at SU 918 460 and take the second signposted bridle-way on your **right**. Follow the route description in paragraphs **2** and **3**, but then turn ← off the NDW and retrace the outward route of the alternative start.

∙ ∙

Pedal power! Climbing the steep escarpment on Hackhurst Downs

Route 2

St Martha's Hill–Abinger loop

START/FINISH	Guildford train station SU 992 496; or Echo Pit Road car park TQ 004 484
DISTANCE	28.5km (17¾ miles)
ON ROAD	7.5km (4¾ miles)
OFF ROAD	21km (13 miles)
ASCENT	550m (1805ft)
GRADE	▲
TIME	4hrs–4hrs 30mins
MAPS	OS Explorer 145, Landranger 186
PUB	The Volunteer Inn, Abinger Hammer
CAFÉ	Abinger Hammer Tearooms

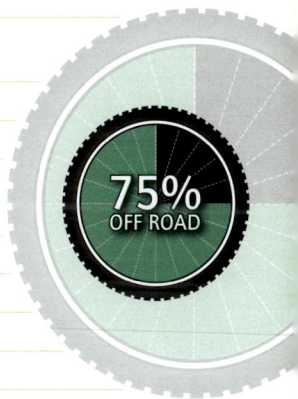

75% OFF ROAD

Overview

Although clocking in at less than 30km, this little gem of a route certainly packs a lot into its relatively modest distance. The route takes in a loop of the wooded and hilly country to the east of Guildford; heading east along the sandy tracks of The Chantries and St Martha's Hill, weaving a route between the villages of Albury, Shere, Gomshall and Abinger Hammer before launching up the steep south escarpment of the North Downs and returning along the bridleways of the NDW. Three-quarters of the route is off road, much of the rest follows narrow country lanes. There are a few climbs to deal with but none so fearsome as the ever-steepening 125m pull up from Hackhurst Farm to the top of the North Downs.

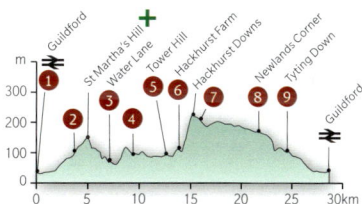

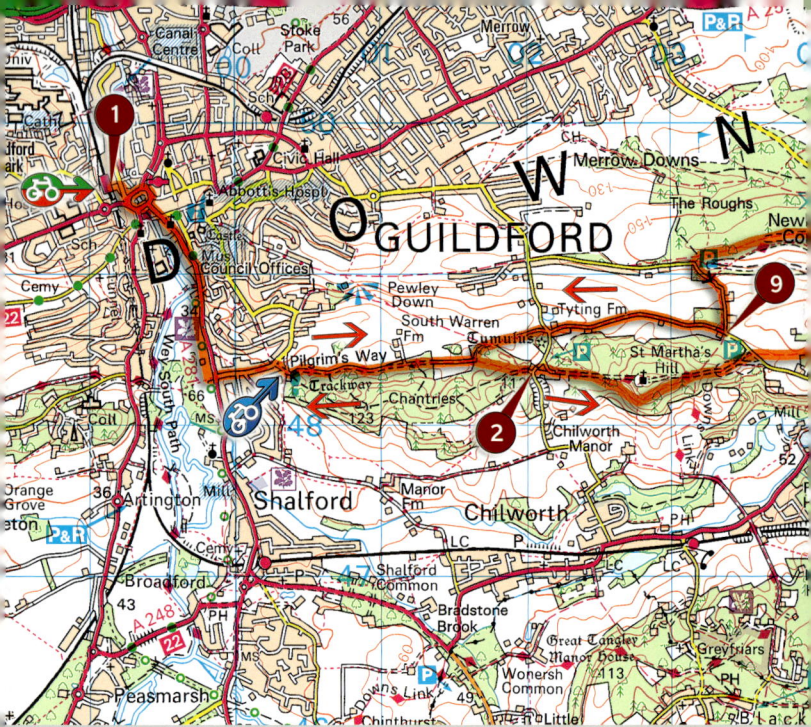

Directions

1 From **Guildford station**, follow the one-way system around to join the `A281` Shalford road. After 650m, join the cycle path running parallel to the **RH** side of the road; follow this for 600m before turning ← (*NDW*) and crossing back over the `A281` onto a residential road. Continue up the road for 400m before turning → onto a track road (*NDW*). Follow the track round past Echo Pit Road car park (an alternative start/finish) as it climbs to the **left** of Chantry Cottage. Continue on this excellent track along the edge of the Chantries woodland. **Beware of an area of soft sand that may stop you in your tracks.**

2 At a T-junction with a minor road (Halfpenny Lane), dogleg ← then → and climb steeply up the flank of **St Martha's Hill** following *NDW* signs. At a fork, the good uphill track becomes footpath only, so turn → and contour around the hill on a frequently unrideable soft sand track. Once the track starts descending you may gain enough traction to stay upright. At a path

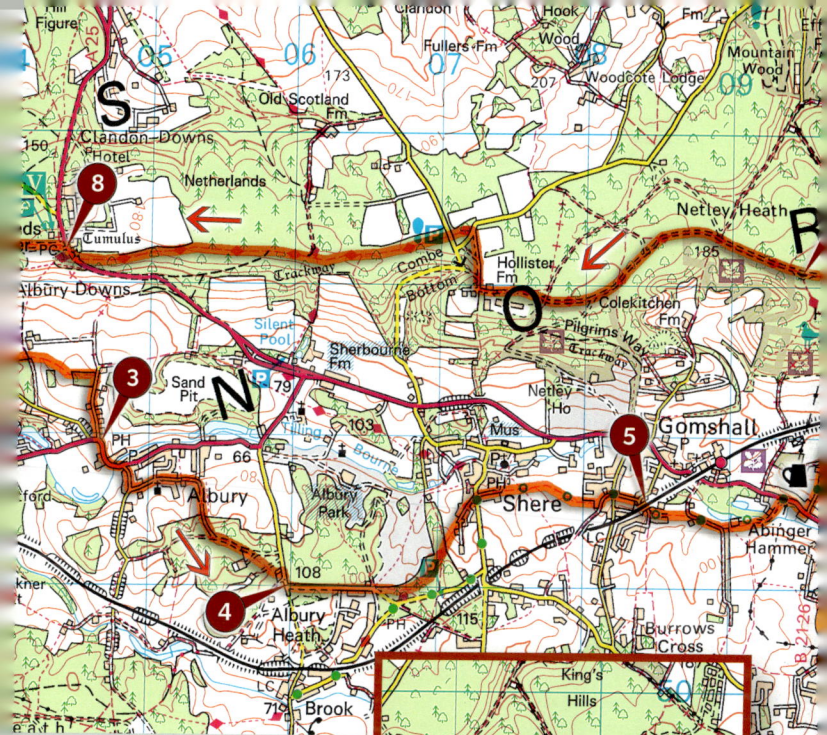

T-junction, keep ↑ along the bridleway. Cross ↑ over the next ✗, passing a *Downs Link* signpost on your right. At a bridleway fork, bear ← to go through a small car park and emerge at a road. Dogleg → then ← onto a narrow, sandy bridleway path to follow the Pilgrim's Way (PW). Keep ↑ at a ✗ and climb across a field before descending steeply down a sunken lane to a ✗. Turn → downhill along Water Lane.

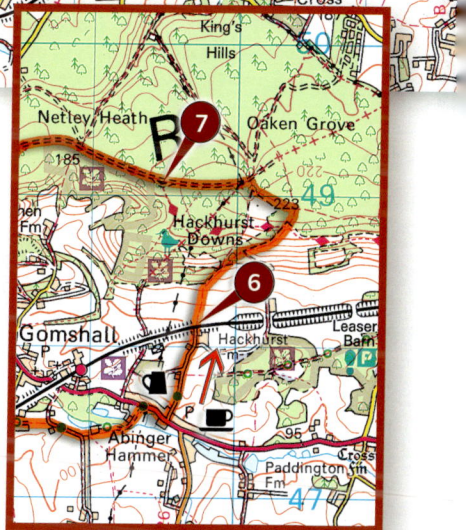

Heading east on the Pilgrim's Way, with Albury Downs beyond

3 At the T-junction with the `A248`, turn ← then after 300m, on entering **Albury**, turn → onto Church Lane opposite the shop/post office. Bear ← at a fork and continue past the **church** and war memorial; the road comes to an end and a track continues ↑ (wooden bridleway signpost) before swinging **right**, uphill between steep embankments. Climb steeply to a T-junction with a broader track, bear ← and continuing climbing. At a fork in a sandy clearing, bear → following a blue bridleway waymarker, then soon bear ← to cross a gravel track and continue ↑ uphill onto a sandy track (bridleway waymarker).

4 On emerging at a road junction, continue ↑ along Park Road (*Peaslake* and *Ewhurst*). After 600m, where the road bends to the right, bear ← onto a bridleway track (wooden signpost) and continue ↑. Follow an old fence then bear → at a fork by a wooden post with bridleway waymarkers. The path soon emerges at the edge of a small housing estate, continue ↑ along Pathfields and at a ✖ on Sandy Lane, cross ↑ onto The Spinning Walk; keep ↑ as tarmac gives way to track. At a T-junction, with Gravelpits Farmhouse to your right, turn ← onto Gravelpits Lane. Continue to a ✖, cross ↑ over Queen Street then bear ← onto High View. At a **LH** bend after 200m, bear → under the railway onto Tower Hill.

5 From **Tower Hill** almost immediately take the second ← entrance onto a broad farm track bridleway. Pass some barns then keep ← through the farmyard. At a T-junction, turn → onto a broad gravel track and at a **RH** bend after 250m, turn ← along a signposted bridleway track, soon forking

→ then ← and continuing ↑. The track joins a concrete road and emerges at the busy `A25`; turn → and continue into **Abinger Hammer**, taking the first ← to climb then descend along Hackhurst Lane. Continue ↑ past **Hackhurst Farm** as tarmac gives way to track. Dismount to cross the railway line through two gates (with caution).

6 Remount and begin the long climb up the ever-steepening north escarpment of **Hackhurst Downs**. In summer, the lower reaches of the path are engulfed by foliage. Where the path forks, keep ↑ (→), climbing steeply. Shortly after the NDW footpath crosses the bridleway the climb levels out; continue ↑ around a gate to the next bridleway ✗. Turn ← onto a path criss-crossed by gnarly tree roots and follow this around to a T-junction with a byway track. Turn ← and continue through a metal gate along a track with a bridleway signpost.

Cruising along the ridge on the North Downs Way at Hackhurst Downs

Negotiating gnarly roots on Hackhurst Downs

7 The bridleway soon joins the NDW; keep ↑ over several ✖ s, passing stables and **Hollister Farm** as the track turns sharply **right** (**N**). Keep ↑ (ignoring two left-hand turns); at Combe Lane, turn → then sharply ← (*North Downs Way*) passing a concrete dew pond. Cross a lane ↑ to go through **West Hanger car park** and continue along the NDW through woodland on a broad track. Arriving at the `A25`, follow the path that leads to the **right**.

8 Cross the `A25` by the Barn Café and continue → through to the far (**W**) end of the large car park at **Newlands Corner**. Exit the car park along a broad bridleway track through woodlands, popping out onto a narrow lane after 1.3km. Turn ← and continue back on yourself along the lane. Where the lane reaches a car park, swing → and descend along Halfpenny Lane. At the bottom, turn → along a bridleway path by Keepers Cottage.

9 Follow the path – **soft sand in places** – through a collection of buildings at **Tyting Farm**, cross ↑ over a lane and follow the bridleway around – ignoring a right fork – to a ✖ at TQ 017 484. Turn → and retrace your outward route to return to **Guildford station**.

Coasting along on a bridleway on Broomy Downs (Route 5)

Routes around Dorking

Woodland bridleway, Hackhurst Downs

Route 3

Hackhurst Downs–Polesden Lacey loop

START/FINISH	Dorking train station TQ 171 504; or Abinger Roughs car park TQ 110 480
DISTANCE	27.5km (17 miles); or 22.5km (14 miles)
ON ROAD	6.5km (4 miles); or 4km (2½ miles)
OFF ROAD	21km (13 miles); or 18.5km (11½ miles)
ASCENT	555m (1820ft); or 480m (1575ft)
GRADE	▲
TIME	2hrs 30mins–3hrs; or 2hrs–2hrs 30mins
MAPS	OS Explorer 145 and 146, Landranger 187
PUB	The Volunteer Inn, Abinger Hammer
CAFÉ	Abinger Hammer Tearooms

75%
OFF ROAD

Overview

For the most part this stimulating route loops around a densely wooded section of the North Downs, west of Dorking. When you're out of the trees, there are some fine views across the beautiful, rolling Surrey countryside. There's also a lot of variety packed into this route's relatively modest distance: there are lengthy woodland sections and the bridleways and byways alternate between sand, chalk, earth and flint; there are a couple of stiff climbs, including a 125m pull up the steep south escarpment of Hackhurst Downs, and some rattling downhills to boot. This route is a great option if you have limited time, but want a ride to get stuck into – and you'll encounter fewer mountain bikers than in the Leith Hill/Holmbury Hill area of the Surrey Hills.

Descending along the Pilgrim's Way trackway below Ranmore Common

Although this route describes a similar loop to Route 4, different bridleways and byways are used for the most part. There are too many quality climbs and descents in this small area to fit into a single route, hence the inclusion of this variation on an excellent theme.

Watch out, slow down for, and give way to horse riders and walkers; the area around Polesden Lacey seems especially popular with dog walkers.

Directions

1 From **Dorking station**, cross to the northbound carriageway of the `A24` and soon turn ← onto the `A2003`, crossing ↑ over a mini roundabout to arrive at a T-junction after 1km. Turn → and follow the road around for 350m before turning ← off the road by a footpath sign just past a large, stone-topped gateway. Just by the footpath sign, join a path on the right indicated by a small, blue National Trust (NT) bridleway sign. This delivers you to an ancient trackway forming part of the **Pilgrim's Way** (PW). Climb steadily and at a ✖ after 1km keep ↑.

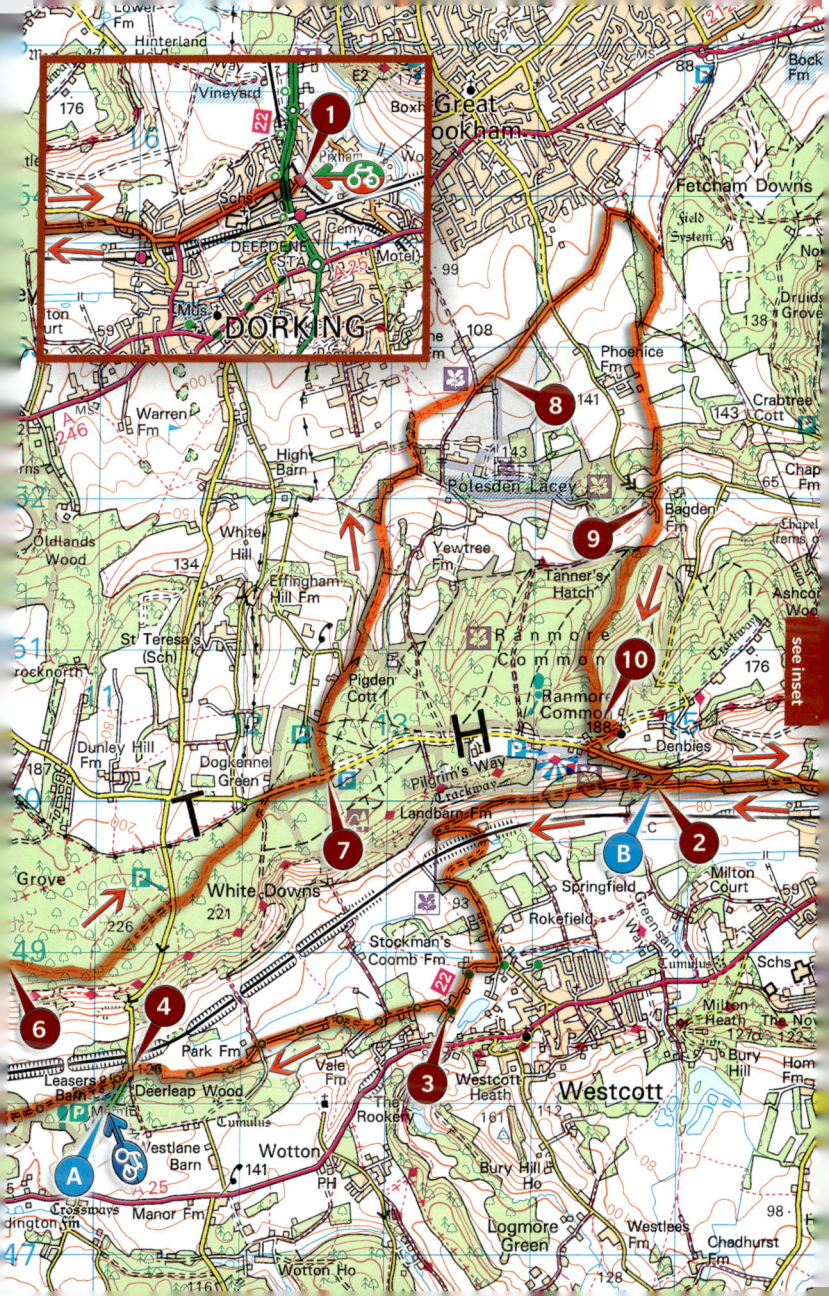

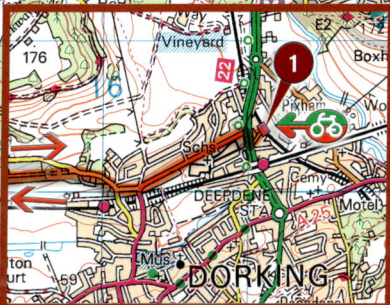

Bishop Wilberforce memorial at Abinger Roughs

② After another 500m turn **←** downhill and descend for 1250m, before the track swings round to the **left** and joins another track. Keep **←** and descend towards **Landbarn Farm**. Pass under the raised railway line and follow the farm road around to join a minor road. Climb along the road over Hole Hill and descend to a T-junction. Turn **→** onto Balchins Lane and follow the road around for 500m, passing a row of houses before turning **→** along a narrow lane (*NCN22* waymarker).

③ Follow the track road around, forking **→** by a bridleway signpost with another *NCN22* waymarker, and continue along the track, keeping **↑** at a **✕** and passing red brick barns at **Park Farm**; after a further kilometre you will arrive at a minor road. Dogleg **←** then **→** across a minor road (White Down Lane) at TQ 113 482 (*NCN22*) and onto a woodland track.

Alternative start from Abinger Roughs car park

Ⓐ Exit the **car park**, turn **←** along White Down Lane and after 300m turn **←** onto a bridleway with an *NCN22* sign.

④ Continue along the woodland bridleway, descend a little then climb briefly over Broomy Downs, keeping **↑** at a **✕**. On arriving at a bridlegate, leave the NCN22, bearing **→** to follow a track down to **Hackhurst Farm**. Pass the farmhouse and turn **→**. Dismount to cross the railway line through two gates (with caution).

⑤ Remount and begin the long climb up the ever-steepening north escarpment of **Hackhurst Downs**. In summer, the lower reaches of the path are thick with foliage. Where the path forks, keep **↑** (**→**) (unless you like a serious challenge, in which case follow the variant route below) climbing quite steeply, eventually crossing **↑** over the NDW. Pass around a gate and continue to a **✕** with a four-way bridleway sign; turn **→**.

Variant route

① Take the **LH** fork and climb the relentlessly steep gradient – can you keep going or will you just run out of gears? At the top of the climb there is a four-way signpost. To the right the NDW is footpath only so follow the bridleway sign pointing **N** and bash your way through the undergrowth for 300m to arrive on a track road. Turn ➔ then ➔ again (bridleway sign) onto a path criss-crossed by gnarly tree roots and follow this around to a ✖ with a four-way bridleway sign; continue ↑.

• •

6 Follow the bridleway (can be churned up in places) as it weaves through woodland, keeping ↑ and ignoring all turnings. Pass an enclosed reservoir and descend a little to a minor road. Cross straight over and continue along a track (can be churned up in places), keeping ↑ at a ✖ before emerging on the Ranmore Common Road. Turn ➔ along the road for 500m, passing a minor

On Hogden Lane byway track

road named Hogden Lane on your left before turning ← onto a (signposted) byway track (also Hogden Lane) shortly after.

7 Begin the long, rattling descent on a flinty track, passing two cottages before the track enters a sunken lane. The descent bottoms out then climbs a little, keep ↑ ignoring bridleways to the right and left and soon follow the track as it leads around to the **left**, ignoring paths leading through gates straight ahead and right. Follow the track round, keeping ↑ over a ✖ then bearing ➔ at a fork. Keep ↑ at another ✖ before emerging on the minor Polesden Road by the North Lodge entrance to **Polesden Lacey House**, a National Trust property.

8 Continue to a ✖ and keep ↑ to join a byway track. At a ✖ after 800m, turn ➔ along an unsignposted bridleway. Pass through a copse, ignore a footpath leading into the woods and bear ➔ to continue along the bridleway for a further 300m before forking ➔ onto another bridleway then climbing steadily alongside Bookham Wood. The path enters the woods and runs between stock fences as it passes by **Phoenice Farm** stables. The path begins descending ever more steeply on the way down through Chapelhill

Wood before emerging (go through the bridlegate) at the top of a meadow. Descend to the obvious bridlegate, go through, then dogleg ← then → across Chapel Lane to continue on a bridleway track (wooden signpost) leading to **Bagden Farm**.

9 Keep ↑ where another bridleway forks right through Bagden Farm and continue to where the track runs out by a wooden farm gate. Go through the bridlegate that sits to the **right** and climb across a meadow to another bridlegate at the edge of the woodland ahead. Enter the woodland and keep ← at a bridleway fork. Climb steadily along the track (often hoof-damaged) and keep ↑ as it merges with another bridleway. At another fork, keep ← (blue NT bridleway marker) and climb more steeply.

10 At the top of the climb the path meets a bridleway T-junction; turn ← and follow the path out to join the road opposite **St Barnabas' Church**. Turn → along the minor road and continue to the T-junction with Ranmore Common Road. Turn ← along the road, looking out for a bridleway on the **right** after 600m. This descends very steeply for 150m before crossing the **PW ancient trackway**; turn ← here to retrace the outward route to **Dorking**.

Alternative finish at Abinger Roughs car park

· ·

B Turn → and continue, climbing steadily along the track for 400m to the top of the ascent, then follow the route description in paragraphs **2** and **3** as far as the minor road at TQ 113 482. Turn ← along the road for 300m to reach the **car park**.

· ·

Old tunnel, Sheepwalk Lane

Route 4

Gomshall–Westhumble loop

START/FINISH	Gomshall train station car park TQ 089 478; or Dorking train station TQ 171 504
DISTANCE	29.75km (18½ miles); or 32.25km (20 miles)
ON ROAD	6km (3¾ miles); or 7.25km (4¼ miles)
OFF ROAD	23.75km (14¾ miles); or 25km (15½ miles)
ASCENT	635m (2080ft); or 710m (2330ft)
GRADE	▲
TIME	3hrs–3hrs 30mins; or 3hrs 15mins–3hrs 45mins
MAPS	OS Explorer 145 and 146, Landranger 187
PUB	The Compasses Inn, Gomshall
CAFÉ	Tillings Café, Gomshall

80% OFF ROAD

Overview

This route explores the byways and bridleways in a fine area of the North Downs around Netley Heath and Ranmore Common, east of Guildford and west of Dorking. The ride begins with a tough climb up to Netley Heath and the NDW. Woodland bridle-

ways and byways take you to Ranmore Common before a rattling descent past Tanner's Hatch YHA leads onto Connicut Lane. A climb and descent bring you out briefly on the Polesden Road before byway and bridleway tracks deliver you to an excellent downhill through Chapelhill Wood. A meander along a country lane to Westhumble restores some calm before the mother of all climbs through Ashcombe Wood tests your mettle. After descending in stages back to the valley floor, the ride back to Gomshall is a relatively relaxing affair. This route is also easily started from Dorking train station (see paragraph Ⓐ).

Directions

1 Exit **Gomshall station** car park and turn → (W) along the `A25`, shortly turning ← along Goose Green by the **Gomshall Mill** pub/restaurant. Follow the road as it leads around to the **left**, continue ↑ past a railway bridge onto High View. Continue to a junction with Queens Lane.

2 At the junction with Queens Lane, cross ↑ onto a bridleway (wooden signpost with an *NCN22* waymarker) along Gravelpits Lane. Bear ← along the track road ignoring a right-hand turn then turn → at a bridleway fork (*NCN22* waymarker) and continue along an earth path. Keep ↑ along the bridleway, which eventually emerges onto tarmac; continue ↑ along the Spinning Walk to a T-junction with Shere Lane, turn → and continue through **Shere**. At a T-junction, dogleg ← then → onto a byway track. Pass a car park (another possible start/finish point) and begin to climb on a broad chalk and flint track. Climb steeply at length, passing under the `A25` – **the path can be very greasy in its lower reaches** – keeping ↑ (→) on the main track where a bridleway forks left.

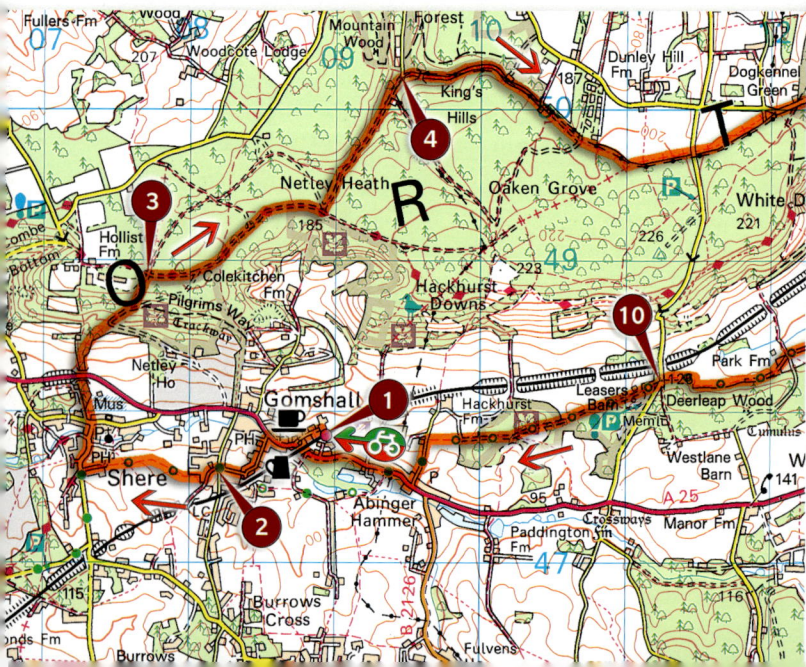

3 Shortly after the climb levels, turn ➜ at a ✖ to join the NDW. Follow the NDW, keeping ⬆ for 1.75km to arrive at a major path junction by a round

Chalk bridleway beneath the steep south escarpment of the North Downs

concrete reservoir at Gravelhill Gate. Turn ← and descend at length along a broad forest track, eventually passing a sawmill.

4 On joining tarmac, turn → onto the Sheepwalk Lane byway track. Keep ↑ along the track for almost 3km – crossing a minor road en route – before emerging on Ranmore Common Road. Turn → and continue along the road for 1.5km, then turn ← onto a bridleway (just to the right of a track with a National Trust sign for Polesden Lacey). There follows a rattling descent – **possible horse hoof damage** – that passes **Tanner's Hatch YHA** before eventually bottoming out then starting to climb along Connicut Lane track. Pass under a fine stone bridge and climb more steeply. The track levels then descends – **possible horse hoof damage** – to emerge at the Polesden Road.

5 Turn → and continue to a ✗ where you keep ↑ to join a byway track. At a ✗ after 800m, turn → along an unsignposted bridleway. Pass through a copse, ignore a footpath leading into the woods and bear → to continue along the bridleway for a further 300m before forking → onto another bridleway then climbing steadily alongside Bookham Wood. The path enters the woods and runs between stock fences as it passes by **Phoenice Farm**. The path begins descending ever more steeply on the way down through Chapelhill

Descending from Chapelhill Wood

Wood before emerging (go through the bridlegate) at the top of a meadow. Descend to the obvious bridlegate, go through, then turn ← along a minor road for 1.2km.

6 Turn → onto a tarmac bridleway by the remains of an ancient **chapel**. Climb steadily along the lane then after 400m fork → onto a narrow bridleway path criss-crossed with tree roots and climb steeply. The path broadens as it enters woodland, but climbs ever more steeply. This is one tough, relentless climb and if you get to the top without putting a foot down – or giving up – you've done well! When the gradient finally eases, keep → at a fork (signpost) to stay on the bridleway. Contour along on a path that can be exceptionally muddy, eventually emerging at a minor road.

7 Turn ← and head towards some large gates with a sign reading *Denbies*. Turn ← by a white barrier and continue along a concrete path (joining the NDW) for a short way before turning → along a bridleway (*NDW*). Descend steadily at first, crossing a ✖ (and leaving the NDW), then more steeply to arrive at Ranmore Road.

Alternative finish at Dorking station

B Turn ← and descend along Ranmore Road. After 800m, where the road levels out beyond a bend, turn ← onto Ashcombe Road. Keep ↑ across a mini roundabout and continue to a T-junction with the `A24`, turn → and take the next ← for **Dorking station**.

Turn → and climb along the road for 500m before turning ← onto a bridleway track and descending steeply for 150m to a ✖ and turn → onto a broad track.

Alternative start from Dorking station

A Cross to the northbound carriageway of the `A24` and soon turn ← onto the `A2003`, crossing ↑ over a mini roundabout to arrive at a T-junction after 1km. Turn → and follow the road around for 350m before turning ← off the road by a footpath sign just past a large, stone-topped gateway. Just by the footpath sign, join a path on the → indicated by a small blue National Trust (NT) bridleway sign. This delivers you to an ancient trackway forming part of the PW. Continue **W** along the track, soon climbing steadily, and continue ↑ at a ✖.

8 Continue to a T-junction and turn ← downhill. Descend for around 1.5km before the track swings round to the **left** and joins another track. Turn → and climb a little, go through a gate and keep ↑ over a ✖. Go through a gate then shortly after turn ← through another gate onto a bridleway. Descend a little, pass under the railway and then dogleg through farm buildings at **Stockman's**.

Loose sand trail near White Down Lane

9 At the T-junction, turn → onto a track road, forking → by a bridleway signpost with an *NCN22* waymarker. Continue along the track, keeping ↑ at a ✗ and passing red brick barns at **Park Farm**; after a further kilometre you will arrive at a minor road. Dogleg ← then → across a minor road (White Down Lane) at TQ 113 482 (*NCN22*) and onto a woodland track.

10 Descend a little then climb briefly over Broomy Downs, keeping ↑ at a ✗. Go through a gate, and then a second gate soon after. Turn ← and descend on tarmac along Hackhurst Lane to **Abinger Hammer**. Turn → and continue along the A25 for 800m to return to **Gomshall station**. Those who started at Dorking station should continue from paragraph **1**.

Climbing Holmbury Hill

5

Route 5

Leith Hill and Holmbury Hill loop

START/FINISH	Dorking train station TQ 171 504; or Abinger Roughs car park TQ 110 480
DISTANCE	33.5km (20¾ miles); or 22.5km (14 miles)
ON ROAD	11.25km (7 miles); or 5km (3 miles)
OFF ROAD	22.25km (13¾ miles); or 17.5km (11 miles)
ASCENT	745m (2445ft); or 550m (1805ft)
GRADE	▲
TIME	3hrs–3hrs 30mins; or 2hrs 30mins–3hrs
MAPS	OS Explorer 145 and 146, Landranger 187
PUB	The Plough at Coldharbour, Abinger Arms at Abinger
CAFÉ	Leith Hill Tower café (weekends only), Abinger Tearooms

65% OFF ROAD

Overview

While staying south of the main ridge of the North Downs, this tough well-rounded ride takes in some of the same highlights as Route 6 – including Leith Hill and Holmbury Hill – although this

is a shorter route and uses different trails wherever possible. Whether starting the route from Dorking or Abinger Roughs, it is something of a three-part ride: a gentle run in on minor roads, lanes and tracks followed by an off-road roller-coaster with a gentle run out at the end.

There are a few uphill and downhill stretches to tackle along the way and the mixed terrain also provides a few challenges – sand, mud, tree roots and broken bricks – to keep you on your toes. Leith Hill and Holmbury Hill are particularly popular with walkers and horse riders as well as mountain bikers, so ride considerately.

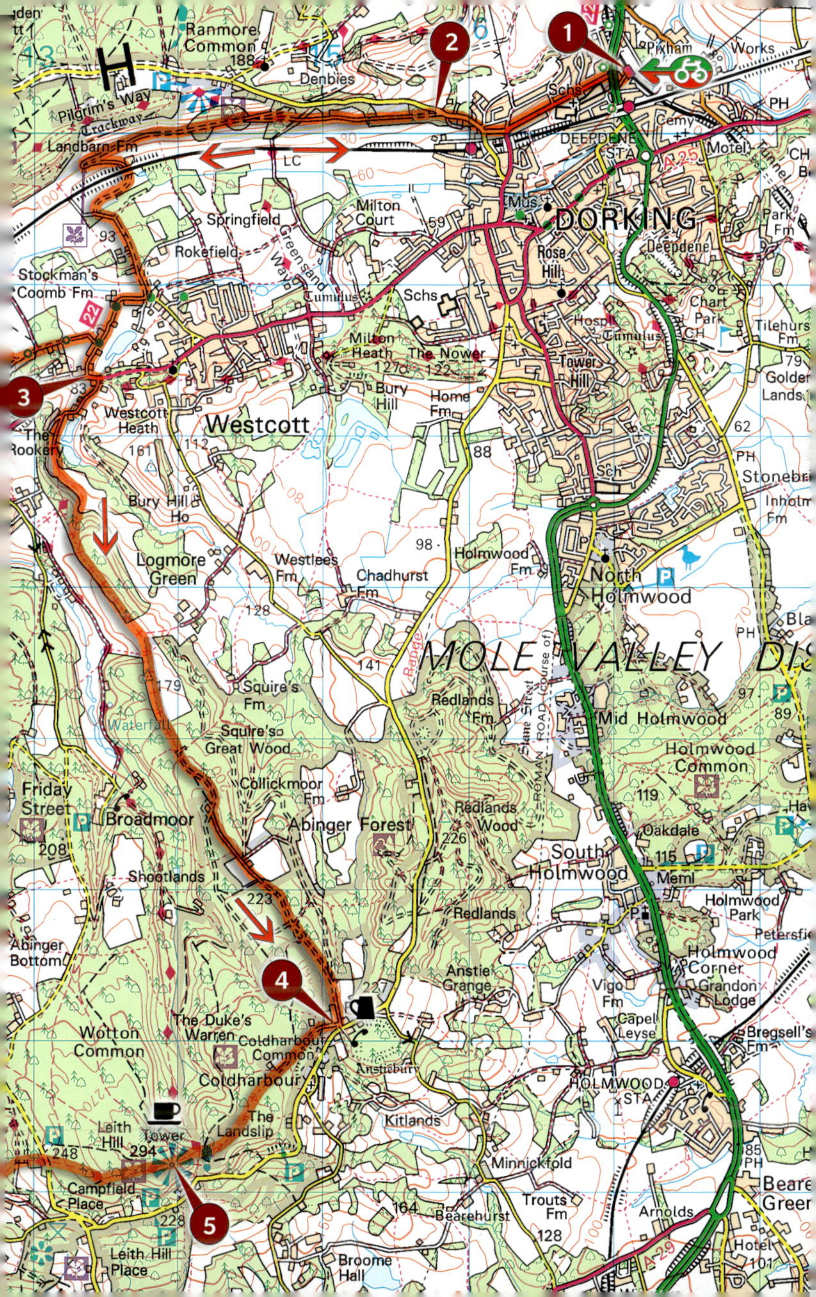

Ranmore Common
188
Denbies
Pilgrim's Way
Trackway
Landbarn Fm
LC
Pixham
Works
PH
Schs
Cemy
DEEPDENE STA
Motel
A25
Tunnel
Mus
DORKING
Deepdene
Park Fm
Springfield
Milton Court
59
Rokefield
Greensand Way
93
Stockman's Coomb Fm
Tumulus
Schs
Rose Hill
Chart Park
CH
Tilehurst Fm
Hospl
Tumulus
Milton Heath
The Nower
127
122
Tower Hill
79
Bury Hill
Home Fm
62
Westcott Heath
Westcott
The Rookery
161
112
88
Sch
PH
Bury Hill Ho
Inholms Fm
98
Logmore Green
Westlees Fm
Holmwood Fm
Chadhurst Fm
North Holmwood
128
141
Range
MOLE VALLEY
PH
Squire's Fm
179
Redlands Fm
Stane Street
ROMAN ROAD (course of)
97
89
Waterfall
Squire's Great Wood
Mid Holmwood
Holmwood Common
Friday Street
Collickmoor Fm
119
Broadmoor
Abinger Forest
Redlands Wood
Oakdale
208
226
South Holmwood
115
Shootlands
Meml
223
Redlands
Holmwood Park
Abinger Bottom
Anstie Grange
Holmwood Corner
227
Grandon Lodge
Vigo Fm
Capel Leyse
Bregsell's Fm
The Duke's Warren
Wotton Common
Coldharbour Common
Coldharbour
Anstiebury
HOLMWOOD STA
Kitlands
The Landslip
Leith Hill Tower
248
294
Minnickfold
85
PH
Campfield Place
164
Bearehurst
Trouts Fm
Arnolds
228
128
Leith Hill Place
Broome Hall
A29
Hotel
101

Directions

1 From **Dorking station**, cross to the northbound carriageway of the `A24` and soon turn ← onto the `A2003`, crossing ↑ over a mini roundabout to arrive at a T-junction after 1km. Turn → and follow the road around for 350m before turning ← off the road by a footpath sign just past a large, stone-topped gateway. Just by the footpath sign, join a path on the **right** indicated by a small blue National Trust (NT) bridleway sign. This delivers you to an ancient trackway forming part of the PW.

2 Continue **W** along the track, soon climbing steadily. Continue ↑ at a ✕ after 1km then after another 500m turn ← downhill at a T-junction and descend for 1.5km, before the track swings round to the **left** and joins another track. Keep ← and descend towards **Landbarn Farm**. Pass under the raised railway line and follow the farm road around to join a minor road. Climb along the road over Hole Hill and descend to a T-junction. Turn → onto Balchins Lane and follow the road around for 800m.

Alternative start from Abinger Roughs car park

A Exit the **car park**, turn ← along White Down Lane and after 300m turn → onto a bridleway with an *NCN22* sign. Continue along the bridleway, keeping ↑ after a ✕ by a brick barn. At a T-junction turn → onto Balchins Lane for 250m.

3 At the next T-junction turn ← onto the busy `A25` (with care) then → after 100m onto Rookery Drive. Follow the private road through a collection of houses, passing Mill House, then turn ← onto a sandy track (*Bridleway*). Follow the track along the edge of woodland then climb steeply to intersect Wolvens Lane. Turn ← and climb along the main track, which is eroded in places by 4x4s and scramble bikes; alternatively, vehicles and large puddles can be avoided by taking to a singletrack path running along the **RH** side of the track. After 4km arrive at a junction with the road by the **Plough Inn** at **Coldharbour**.

4 Turn → and climb along a wide gravel track (*Byway*), soon forking → (*Tower*). Climb steeply, pass a cricket field then fork ←. After 800m arrive at a ✕ of tracks, turn → downhill (green-topped marker post) and soon come to a multiple track junction. Turn ← and climb very steeply uphill by a four-way signpost, negotiating some gnarly roots before arriving at the summit of **Leith Hill** (294m).

5 Pass the tower and continue **W** on the **Greensand Way** (GW) (a separate path for walkers runs parallel to the main track), descending to Leith Hill Road. Dogleg → then ← across the road to a small parking area to rejoin the GW (wooden signpost). Descend along the bridleway and keep ↑ where the GW bears right. At a ✗ , continue descending ↑ (**W**) along a fairly bumpy track. Where a locked gate bars the main track, turn ← over a small bridge onto a parallel bridleway. The path narrows along a field edge before you dogleg ← then → through **Upfolds Farm**.

6 At the T-junction with the B2126 , turn ← and after 250m turn → onto a bridleway (wooden signpost), cross two streams and climb steeply past a house named **Joldwynds** before emerging on another minor road. Turn ← along the road, continue past **Holmbury House** and turn → at a junction. Climb along the road for 500m then turn → off the road by a small parking

The top of the climb on Holmbury Hill

area onto a short, steep sandstone track. Where the track levels it is often a quagmire. Negotiate this and continue to a major ✖ with a stone cairn and plaque reading 'Hurtwood Millennium Pinetum'. Take the track that sits immediately to the **right** of this and descend steadily **NNE**, keeping ↑ for 2km until you reach a T-junction by a small pond. Turn → and follow the track up a slope, keeping ↑ (←) at a fork. Cross a car park by Holmbury St Mary YHA and descend on a minor road through a sunken lane.

7 Turn ← on the `B2126` and follow the winding road for 2.5km to **Abinger Hammer**. Turn ← onto the `A25` at the T-junction, then turn → just past the building with an ornate clock tower to climb along a narrow lane (*no through road*). At the brow of the hill turn → onto a bridleway (*NCN22*) and follow the narrow path next to a stock fence to a bridlegate. Go through and continue on a broad woodland track across Broomy Downs; at a ✖ keep ↑ (*NCN22*) to arrive at a minor road (White Down Lane). (Turn → here for the alternative finish at Abinger Roughs **car park**.)

8 At White Down Lane, dogleg ← then → across the road to continue along the bridleway (*NCN22*). Keep ↑ after a ✖ by a brick barn then at a T-junction turn ← onto Balchins Lane. Retrace the route back to Dorking station by following Balchins Lane as it leads around a **right** bend, and turn ← to climb

On the level on Holmbury Hill

Woodland singletrack on Holmbury Hill

up and over Hole Hill. At a bend, turn ➔ through a gate and follow the farm road under the railway line; turn ⬅ by Landbarn Farm and climb steadily for 350m before turning ➔ onto the PW. Climb steadily for 1.5km, fork ➔ and descend along the PW. Just before a gate at the bottom of the descent, turn ➔ and follow the path out onto the Ranmore Road; turn ➔ and shortly turn ⬅ onto Ashcombe Road (A2003). Keep ⬆ across a mini roundabout and continue to a T-junction with the A24; turn ➔ and take the next ⬅ for **Dorking station**.

Woodland singletrack on Holmbury Hill

6

Route 6

Surrey Hills Grand Traverse

START/FINISH	Abinger Roughs car park **TQ 110 480**; or Dorking train station **TQ 171 504**
DISTANCE	41.5km (25¾ miles); or 54km (33½ miles)
ON ROAD	6.5km (4 miles); or 9.75km (6 miles)
OFF ROAD	35km (21¾ miles); or 44.25km (27½ miles)
ASCENT	1010m (3315ft); or 1205m (3955ft)
GRADE	◆
TIME	4hrs–4hrs 30mins; or 5hrs, 30mins–6hrs
MAPS	OS Explorer 145 and 146, Landranger 187
PUB	The Plough at Coldharbour; The Royal Oak, Holmbury St Mary; The Hurtwood Inn, Peaslake
CAFÉ	Leith Hill Tower café (weekends only); Abinger Tearooms, Peaslake Village Stores

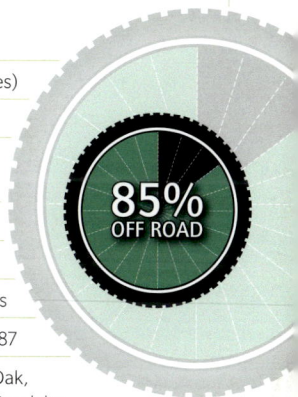

85%
OFF ROAD

Overview

As the title suggests, this magnificent and challenging route takes in a sizeable swathe of the Surrey Hills AONB, stitching together a series of fine bridleways, byways and narrow country lanes to make for an exceptional day out on the trails. The summits of Leith Hill, Holmbury Hill and Pitch Hill are all visited, as is the main ridge of the North Downs. The varied terrain includes sand, earth, chalk and flint bridleways and byways, woodland singletrack with berms and jumps (which can be avoided) as well as metalled farm tracks and tarmacked lanes. There's a significant amount of climbing and descending – you'll be feeling it in your legs before the day is through.

Unsurprisingly, this is a very popular area with walkers and horse riders as well as mountain bikers; from spring through summer and autumn the trails can be very busy, especially at weekends. Please be aware that dogs are allowed to exercise freely, without leads, on The Hurtwood. The village of Peaslake lies at the heart of Surrey Hills mountain biking country and the trinity of hills roundabout is something of a Holy Grail for riders from all over the south of England and beyond.

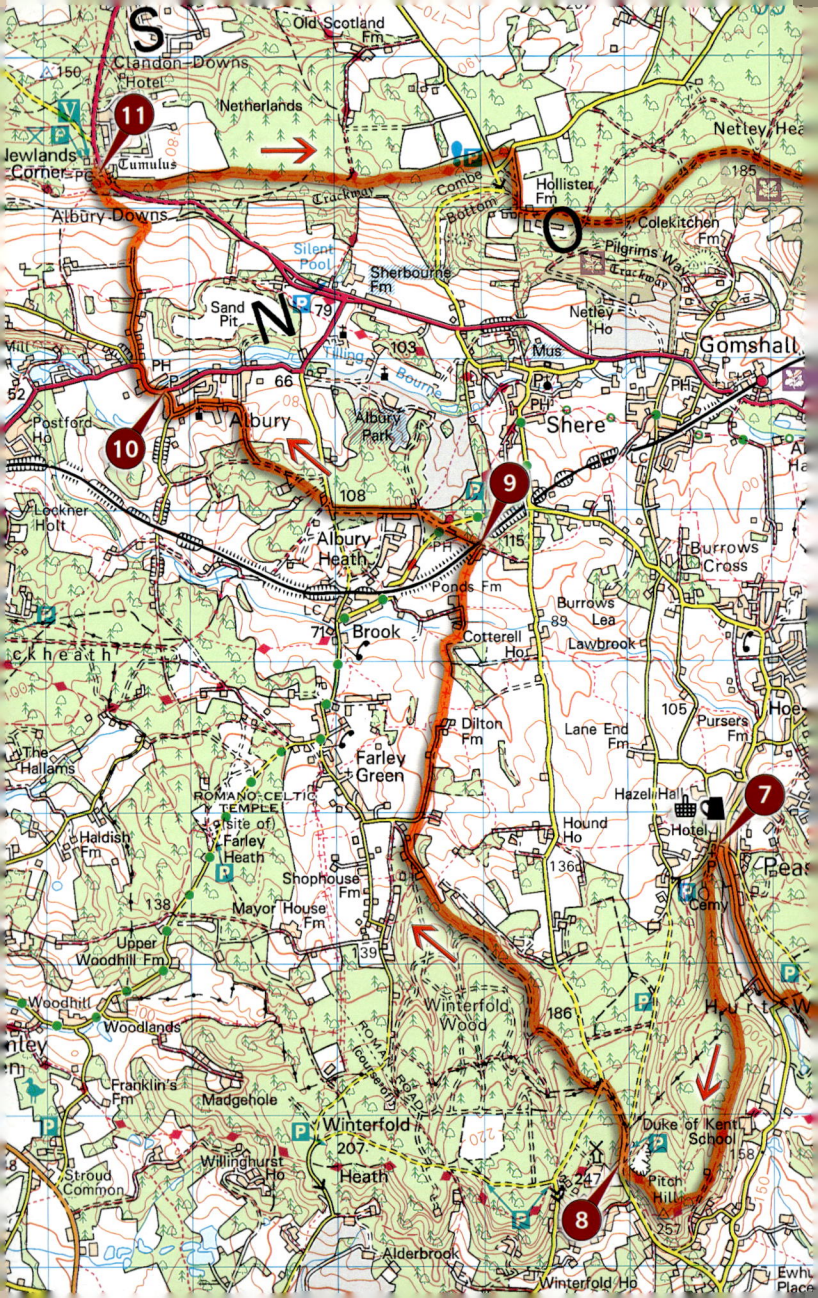

map continues on p.72

Directions

Alternative start from Dorking station

A Cross to the northbound carriageway of the A24 and soon turn ← onto the A2003, crossing ↑ over a mini roundabout to arrive at a T-junction after 1km. Turn → and follow the road around for 350m before turning ← off the road by a footpath sign just past a large, stone-topped gateway. Just by the footpath sign, join a path on the **right** indicated by a small, blue National Trust (NT) bridleway sign. This delivers you to an ancient trackway forming part of the PW.

B Continue **W** along the track, soon climbing steadily. Continue ↑ at a ✗ after 1km then after another 500m turn ← downhill at a T-junction and descend a similar distance, before the track swings round to the **left** and joins another track. Keep ← and descend towards **Landbarn Farm**. Pass under the raised railway line and follow the farm road around to join a minor road. Climb along the road over Hole Hill and descend to a T-junction. Turn → onto Balchins Lane and follow the road around for 800m (then follow the route description in paragraph **2**).

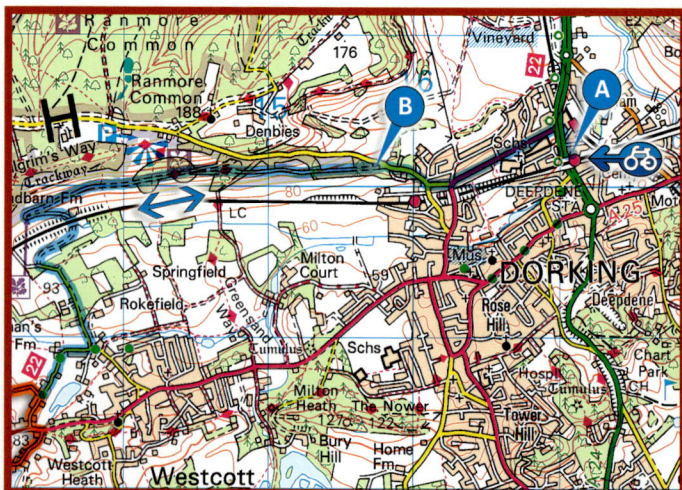

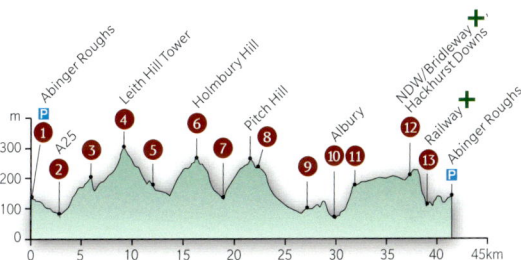

1 Exit the **car park**, turn ← along White Down Lane and after 300m turn → onto a bridleway (*NCN22*). Continue along the bridleway keeping ↑ after a ✗ by a brick barn. At a T-junction turn → along Balchins Lane.

2 At the next T-junction turn ← onto the busy `A25` (with care) and then turn → after 100m onto Rookery Drive. Follow the private road through a collection of houses, passing Mill House, then turn → onto a sandy track (*Bridleway*). Follow the track along the edge of woodland then climb steeply to intersect Wolvens Lane. Turn ← and climb along the main track, which is eroded in places by 4x4s and scramble bikes. Continue for 1.75km.

3 Turn → onto a signposted bridleway (low barrier across path) and continue ↑ to soon descend steeply through Simons Copse. Shortly after the track bottoms out it intersects the GW; turn ← and continue along the GW, initially on tarmac. Keep ↑ (→) ignoring the left-hand fork by Tilling Springs; on passing Warren Farm, tarmac gives way to the sandstone of Whiteberry Road, which soon climbs more steeply. On arriving at a ✗ of tracks, turn ← and climb very steeply uphill by a four-way signpost, negotiating some gnarly tree roots before arriving at the summit of **Leith Hill** (294m).

4 Pass the tower and continue **W** on the **GW** (a separate path for walkers runs parallel to the main track), descending to the Leith Hill Road where you should dogleg → and then ← across the road to the near end of a small parking area to rejoin the GW (wooden signpost). Descend along the bridleway and at a ✗ turn → along the GW. After 400m at a ✗ turn ← to stay on the GW, contouring and descending for 1.6km to arrive at **Pasture Wood** road.

Climbing through Pasture Wood

5 Turn ← and shortly arrive at a T-junction. Turn → along Horsham Road and continue for 1.5km through **Holmbury St Mary** (turn → at the small green in front of **The Royal Oak**) before turning ← into a **parking area** at **TQ 108 451**. From the car park, follow the bridleway that climbs fairly steeply **S**. After 1.5km keep ↑ (**S**) over a ✘ to rejoin the GW, which forks **right** after 250m, leading to the summit of **Holmbury Hill** (261m).

The Surrey Hills and Kent Downs – the home of the country pub

6 From the summit trig point, descend **NW** (→) along the obvious path, keeping ← at a fork before turning ← onto a forestry track (GW), then keeping ← at a ✘ to arrive at a **parking area**. Head for the top **RH** corner of the car park and join a singletrack path through the woods. Watch out for a **LH** fork 150m before the main path joins a forestry track and follow this excellent section of singletrack – there are a few jumps, all of which can be bypassed – which eventually switchbacks into a descent with excellent berms before spitting you out on the Ewhurst Road, south of Peaslake. Turn → and continue for 1km into **Peaslake**.

7 Turn ← past the memorial, pass the hotel and bike hire shop then immediately turn ← (wooden bridleway signpost). Climb past a small church and enter woodland, soon passing to the left of a **cemetery**. Continue climbing steadily, keeping ↑ (←) at a fork before joining the GW as the bridleway climbs to the trig point in a clearing at the summit of **Pitch Hill** (257m). Bear → (**NW**) and continue along the GW – a permissive footpath at this point – soon descending past a quarry before emerging onto a narrow lane at Ride Way. Pitch Hill is part of The Hurtwood, in which mountain bikers have the 'right to roam' on footpaths, unless there are signs specifically excluding bikes and subject to the Bikers' Code (see 'Rights of Way and other users'; p23).

8 Turn → and continue along the lane, keep ← at a fork, then after 400m turn ← onto another minor road (*Winterfold*) and almost immediately turn → again onto a bridleway entering woodland (just before a large metal gateway). Descend along the track through **Winterfold Wood**, keeping ↑ at a bridleway ✗. Continue ↑ on the bridleway along a sunken lane (the track can be wildly wet and muddy in places) and where it emerges from the woods turn → at the fork, soon passing Lockhurst Hatch Farm on the Ponds Lane track. After 2km, the track comes to a **railway crossing**; dismount and cross the railway line (with care) through gates either side.

Trying to keep traction through a quagmire in Winterfold Wood

9 Remount and continue **NW** along the main track, keeping → at a fork to arrive at a ✗ of minor roads. Continue ↑ (**NW**) and follow New Road (*Albury* and *Guildford*) along to a T-junction. Cross over the junction onto a track road then cross ↑ over an intersecting track road and join a bridleway (wooden signpost) next to a house. Continue through woodland, keeping → at a fork along Warren Lane. Descend along a sunken lane and continue following the bridleway as it swings **left** at a ✗, soon emerging onto a residential road. Continue along Church Lane into **Albury**, passing the **church** and war memorial. Stay with the lane as it bends sharply **right** then, at a T-junction, turn ← onto the A248 opposite the post office.

10 Follow the road around a bend and just as it bends again, turn → and begin climbing along Water Lane. Continue ↑ to pass some farm buildings, before the minor road gives way to track and climbs more steeply. The chalk track passes an old pit, swings **left** and continues climbing quite steeply for another 500m. Just before reaching the car park at **Newlands Corner**, turn

➜ on a narrower path and cross the `A25` to join the NDW (wooden *LDP* signpost) where it enters woodland along an old drove road heading **E**.

11 Follow the track along the ridge for 2.5km before reaching **West Hanger car park**, continue ↑ across Staple Lane (*NDW*) and along a woodland bridleway to arrive at Combe Lane. Turn ➜ (*NDW*), then almost immediately ← and continue ↑ along a bridleway track, which turns sharply **left** (*NDW*) through **Hollister Farm** and (forking **right**) re-enters woodland on a partly surfaced track. Keep ↑ over a ✕ and continue through Netley Park and Netley Heath for 2km keeping ↑ on the NDW at ✕s. Continue ↑ on the main track where the NDW becomes footpath and forks **right** at **Hackhurst Downs**.

12 After a further 600m, pass through an old gateway and turn ➜ (bridleway marker) onto a path criss-crossed by gnarly tree roots and follow this around to a ✕ with a four-way bridleway sign. Turn ➜ to descend a bridleway through Hackhurst Downs, passing around a gate. Keep ↑ as the bridleway

Climbing along Water Lane

merges with another bridleway and continue descending (the path can be overgrown in summer) to arrive at a railway crossing at the foot of the escarpment.

⑬ Dismount to cross the **railway line** through two gates (with caution). Continue ↑ through **Hackhurst Farm**. Turn ← past the farmhouse along a track. Keep → where the track forks and climb a little to a T-junction with a bridleway by a bridlegate. Turn ← to continue on a broad woodland track across Broomy Downs. At a ✕ keep ↑ (*NCN22*). Arriving at a minor road, turn → to return to Abinger Roughs **car park**.

Alternative finish at Dorking station

Ⓒ Dogleg ← then → across the minor road to continue along the bridleway (*NCN22*). Keep ↑ after a ✕ by a brick barn then at a T-junction turn ← onto Balchins Lane. Retrace the route back to Dorking station by following Balchins Lane as it leads around a **right** bend, and turn ← to climb up and over Hole Hill. At a bend, turn → through a gate and follow the farm road under the railway line; turn ← by **Landbarn Farm** and climb steadily for 350m before turning → onto the PW. Climb steadily for 1.5km, fork → and descend along the PW. Just before a gate at the bottom of the descent, turn → and follow the path out onto the Ranmore Road; turn → and shortly turn ← onto Ashcombe Road (**A2003**). Keep ↑ across a mini roundabout and continue to a T-junction with the **A24**; turn → and take the next ← for **Dorking station**.

The steep chalk track ascent of Colley Hill (Route 8)

Routes around **Reigate and Redhill**

Singletrack trail on the Greensand Way

7

Route 7

Oxted and Bletchingley loop

START/FINISH	Oxted train station TQ 393 529
DISTANCE	24km (15 miles)
ON ROAD	9.5km (6 miles)
OFF ROAD	14.5km (9 miles)
ASCENT	615m (2020ft)
GRADE	■
TIME	3hrs–3hrs 30mins
MAPS	OS Explorer 146, Landranger 187
PUB	The Barley Mow, Tandridge; various in Oxted and Bletchingley
CAFÉ	Café Papillon, Oxted

60%
OFF ROAD

Overview

This sinuous route snakes its way through the east Surrey countryside, crossing and recrossing the infamous London Orbital – the M25 – with the M23 forming its western boundary. Despite the proximity of these motorways and several large conurbations, the collection of paths, tracks and minor roads linked together here take in some fine scenery and are often so quiet that at times you will feel a long way away from the southeast of England's densely populated urban sprawl.

A first outing will require some attention to navigation, but the route will become familiar with repeat outings. Stretches of the Greensand Way and NDW are incorporated in the route and there is one very big climb up the steep south escarpment of the North Downs near the start, which makes for a real lung-busting challenge.

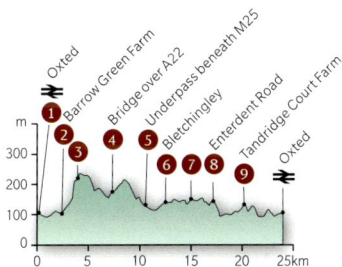

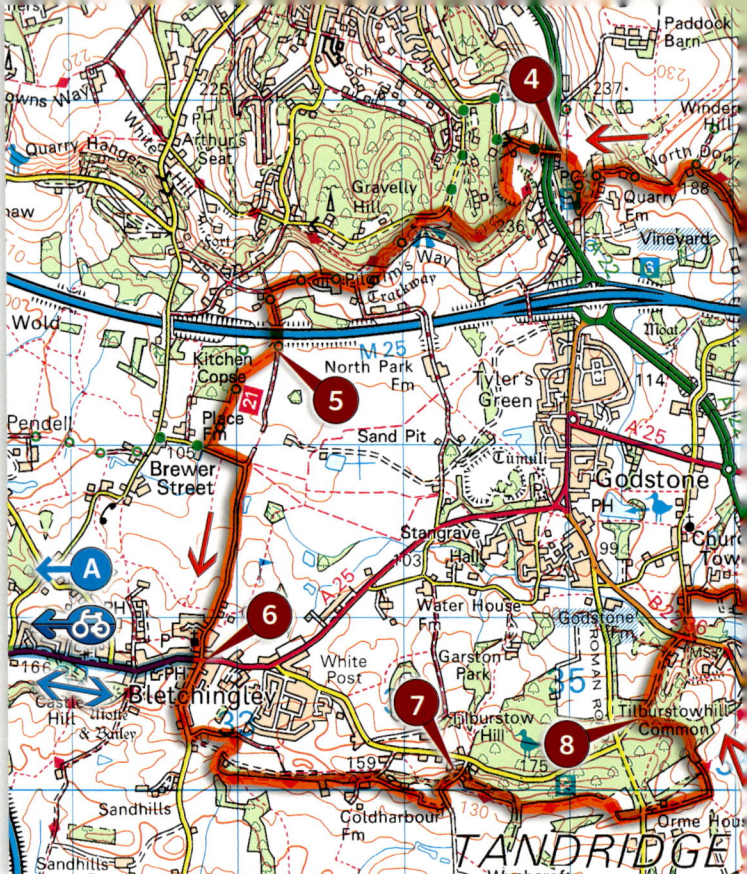

Directions

1 From **Oxted station** head **SW** along Station Road West, continue ↑ over a roundabout to join Church Lane. After 600m arrive at a T-junction and bear → onto the busy **A25** and take the next ← onto the High Street. Continue through **Old Oxted** for 250m then at a ✖ by The Old Bell pub, turn → onto Brook Lane – which soon becomes Sandy Lane. At a T-junction, turn ← along Barrow Green Road, and continue for 300m.

2 Turn ➔ onto a driveway (*Barrow Green Farm*). Follow the bridleway track between fences topped with razor wire and bristling with CCTV cameras – the frequently advertised guard dogs may also make you aware of their presence. Moving swiftly on, cross a bridge high above the `M25` and bear ⬅ along a bridleway track approaching the very steep south escarpment of the North Downs. Climb ever more steeply on a narrow, fenced path with a few roots for added interest; you will be doing well to get to the top of the climb without getting (or falling) off and pushing. In winter particularly it can be impossible to ride this bridleway in its upper reaches due to hoof damage.

3 At a ✖ with a signpost (*NDW/Woldingham Countryside Walk*), turn ← and climb steeply a short way. Turn ← again (*North Downs Way*) then join a minor road that bears **left**. Continue ↑ ignoring a left-hand fork after 300m. Climb a little then descend around a **LH** bend passing a ✖ with the NDW; as the descent steepens, turn sharp → along a broad track (*Bridleway*). At a T-junction, bear ← to join the **NDW**. The track becomes concrete and then tarmac as you approach a large factory/warehouse; where a signpost indicates *NCN21* head ← downhill past the factory, soon turning sharp → (*NCN21*), and climb steadily along a broad track for 400m.

4 Turn ← to cross a bridge over the `A22` and then continue ↑ to climb steeply along a tarmac lane. After 150m, turn ← onto a bridleway with a bollard at its entrance. Continue along the path, which soon broadens as it joins the NDW (bear →) and climbs a little through woodland. At a T-junction with the road by Caterham Viewpoint, turn ← and after 150m, bear ← onto a track (*North Downs Way/NCN21*). Descend, keep ← at a fork (the right-hand option is the NDW) and continue downhill following the *NCN21* signpost – follow the NDW and take the **RH** fork. Bear → at a ✖ shortly after, following the *NCN21* signs. Descend past a house and then turn ← at a ✖ and continue downhill.

5 Go through an underpass beneath the `M25`. Follow the track as it leads around to the **right** and skirts a large excavation site. Keep following the gravel track around the perimeter of the site (*NCN21*) and, where the NCN21 exits (right) onto a minor road, turn ← and continue around a **RH** bend. Climb a little along Church Lane into **Bletchingley**.

Alternative start/finish at Redhill station

A The route can also be started from Redhill station – just follow the `A25` for 5km to **Bletchingley**, turn → onto Outwood Lane at a ✖ in the centre of the village and follow the route description from paragraphs **6** to **9** until you reach the `A25` crossing at the Old Bell Pub. From here go ↑ to follow Brook Lane as in paragraph **1**, and follow the route description from this point to the end of paragraph **5**. At the crossing with the `A25`, turn → and continue for 5km back to **Redhill**.

6 At the ✖ with the `A25`, cross ↑ over and continue along Outwood Lane. After 500m, once you are beyond the houses, turn ← then immediately bear ← around a metal gate onto the GW on a bridleway (wooden signpost),

Metalled track near Leigh Place

Rhododendron woods near Tandridge Court

passing a pond and soon arriving at a ✖. Turn → and descend on a rough narrow path, passing between two concrete pillars. At the next ✖ keep ↑ downhill, passing to the ← of a metal gate before the track levels out. Continue ↑ and soon climb steeply. Keep → at a fork at the top of the ascent, then descend. The bridleway doglegs before intersecting a minor road; turn ← and climb for 250m.

7 Turn → along the GW (*Bridleway*). Continue along a broad track through woodland; at a ✖ jink → then ← to continue (**E**) along the GW to the left of large paddocks. Climb gently then descend to a minor road. Cross ↑ over the road and go through a metal gate to continue on the GW. Descend around a long bend then keep ↑ on the bridleway where the GW forks off to the right as a footpath. Pass around a metal gate and climb steadily along a horse chestnut-lined sunken lane crossing **Tilburstowhill Common**.

8 At a T-junction with the singletrack Enterdent Road, turn → and descend fairly steeply to a T-junction with the `B2236`. Dogleg → then ← to continue along Church Lane. After 250m turn → for **Leigh Place** along a narrow lane (no through road) with a bridleway signpost. Tarmac soon gives way to track; pass around a gate with a sign for *Hop Garden Cottage*, go through an underpass and at a ✖ by the cottage, turn → and continue along a good track. On arriving opposite a large house called The Dairy on Jackass Lane, turn → and continue to the T-junction.

9 At the T-junction with Tandridge Lane, dogleg ← then → onto a driveway at **Tandridge Court Farm** (farm shop signs) and continue along the bridleway, which soon becomes a track. Pass beneath a footbridge and climb steadily alongside a wall with overhanging rhododendrons. The path soon levels and can be fairly muddy for much of the year. Keep ↑ (→) where the bridleway joins a minor road and descend to a T-junction with a wider road. Turn ← and climb then descend to arrive at a ✖ with the `A25` in **Oxted** opposite The Old Bell pub. Turn → along the High Street, swinging ← to a T-junction with the `A25` after 200m. Turn → (with care) along the `A25` a short way before turning ← onto Church Lane (*Oxted Town Centre*). After 600m keep ↑ over a roundabout and continue along Station Road West to return to the **station**.

The steep chalk track descent from Colley Hill

8

Route 8
Box Hill–Banstead Heath loop

START/FINISH	Reigate train station TQ 254 507
DISTANCE	29.75km (18½ miles)
ON ROAD	5.5km (3½ miles)
OFF ROAD	24.25km (15 miles)
ASCENT	635m (2085ft)
GRADE	▲
TIME	3hrs 30mins–4hrs
MAPS	OS Explorer 146, Landranger 187
PUB	The Tree, Box Hill; The Blue Ball, Walton on the Hill
CAFÉ	Box Tree Café, Box Hill; The Grey Dove Tearoom, Walton on the Hill

80%
OFF ROAD

Overview

Your legs will be barely warmed up before the frontal assault on the exceedingly steep southern escarpment of the North Downs flanking Colley Hill. The NDW leads you out on an entertaining canter westwards along the ridge to Box Hill, with just a few minor uphill and downhill sections, allowing plenty of time to recover. A long and exhilarating downhill swoop to Juniper Bottom is followed by a long, steady climb up to Mickleham Downs then an arrow-straight ride out along Stane Street Roman Road across the M25 to Langley Vale. This marks the furthest limit of the route's northwards incursion before the return leg heads across country to Walton on the Hill, then across Banstead Heath back to the NDW. Test your brakes before heading back down the hill into Reigate!

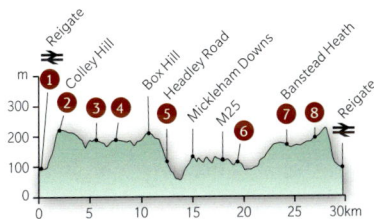

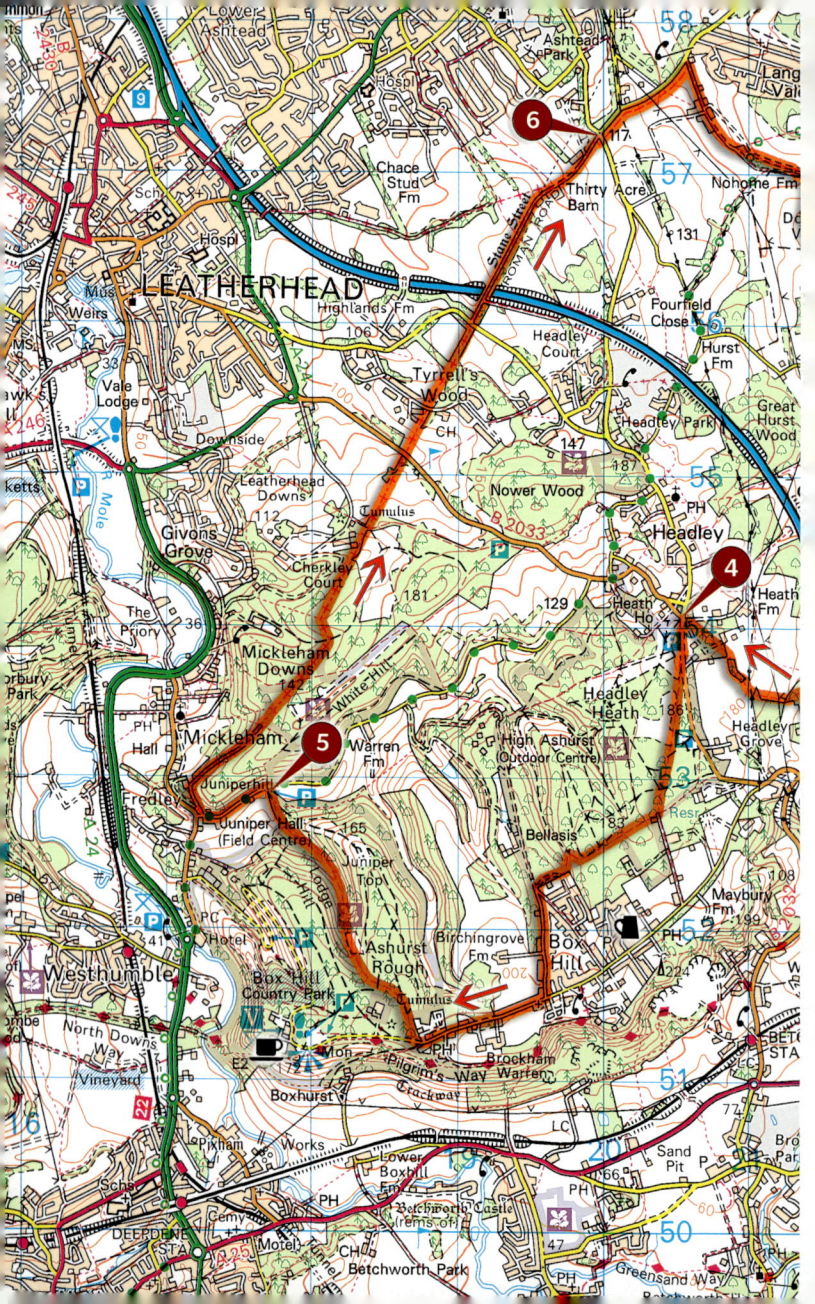

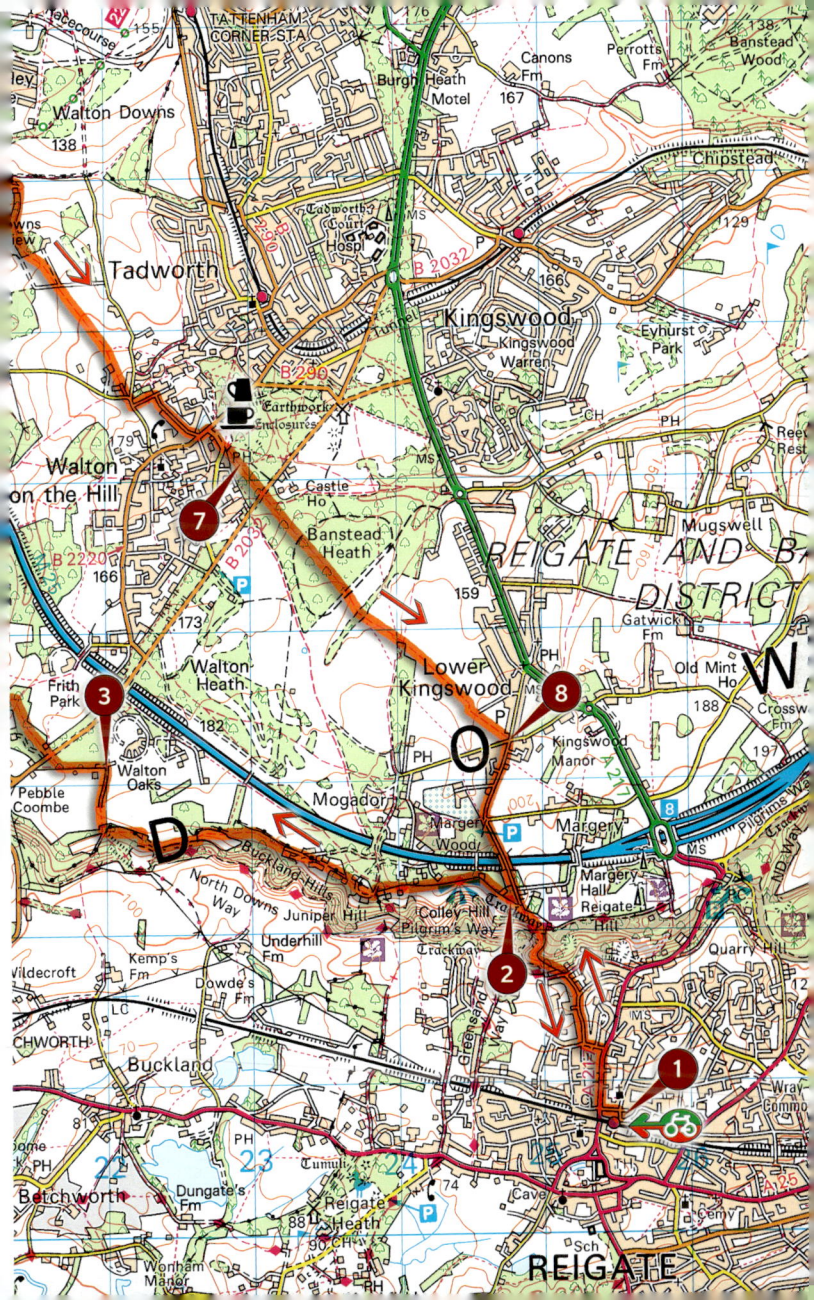

Directions

1 From **Reigate station**, turn → onto the busy `A217`. After 500m, turn ← onto Brokes Road, bearing right onto Beech Road at a fork. Climb steadily along Beech Road for 350m before forking ← onto Underhill Park Road. At a bend after 200m, fork → onto a broad chalk bridleway path. Climb steeply at first then very, very steeply, passing a trig point-shaped memorial stone before arriving at a gate. Go through and continue on a gentle rise to the top of the escarpment on **Colley Hill**. Continue along the path to a ✗ and turn ← to follow the NDW.

2 Follow the NDW for just over 1km to a ✗ by Mole Place and turn → along a bridleway (note that the NDW turns left here to drop steeply down the escarpment; there is a warning sign). Continue along the bridleway, which is hemmed in by high fences on both sides before eventually emerging into woodland. The path turns sharp **left**, drops, turns sharp **right** then contours along before a short sharp climb. Continue through woodland to a ✗, turn → and climb briefly along a byway track.

3 Around 400m after the track levels, turn ← along a bridleway (there may be no signpost). Continue through woodland at Little Heath, bearing → at a fork before crossing a road and continuing ↑ on a bridleway (wooden signpost). Keep ← at a fork then ← again at a second fork and climb a little along a sunken lane that **may be horse hoof damaged**. Bear ← at a fork by an NT sign (*Headley Heath*), continue across a private road in front of a house named White Lodge and shortly emerge on Headley Common Road.

4 Cross Headley Common Road and turn ← to follow a broad bridleway path. Go through gates, continue ↑ over a bridleway ✗ and at a second ✗ by a house, turn → and follow an often-muddy roller-coasting bridleway through the woods. Keep to the main track, which does a zig and then a zag before eventually emerging at a parking area on a track road. Turn ← then fork → to follow the track road between houses before arriving at **Box Hill** road. Turn → and follow the road for 1km before turning → onto a bridleway leading into woodland at **Box Hill Country Park**. Continue along the bridleway and at a major ✗ keep ↑ and begin descending steeply along a fast flint and chalk track. This is an excellent descent, which seems to go on forever along Juniper Bottom.

The view west along the North Downs escarpment from Colley Hill

5 Eventually the descent spits you out at a car park on Headley Road. Turn ← along the road and after 500m, turn → (wooden signpost) then immediately fork → onto the Downs Road byway (no motor vehicles sign) – which follows the course of **Stane Street Roman Road** – and begin climbing steeply on the chalk and flint track. The gradient eases, then at a fork with a path with a barrier across it, bear ← to continue on the byway to continue across the **Mickleham Downs**. Descend and continue to a T-junction of paths. Turn ← – a Thames Down Link path signpost indicates *Thirty Acre Barn 2 miles* – and continue along the byway, which roller-coasters along, crossing a minor road then climbing again and crossing another road before passing high above the M25 on a bridge. Continue on the byway, joining a surfaced road by stables before arriving at a ✖.

6 Cross ↑ and follow the road for 800m down towards **Langley Vale**. Turn → onto a bridleway track road (wooden signpost – *2¼ miles Walton on the Hill*) and continue through Langley Bottom Farm. The road gives way to earth track; keep ↑ and ignore all turns until you reach **Nohome Farm**. Turn → on the bridleway past the house, climbing steeply at first then more steadily along a gravel track. The path climbs steadily for what seems like an eternity before emerging at a road by a junction; continue ↑ along Hurst Road a short way before turning ← on a byway track (wooden signpost) for a short way. Emerge at a junction of residential streets, turn → and continue along

The long descent from Box Hill along Juniper Bottom

Sandlands Road. At a T-junction, turn ← to pass a large pond, then take the next **RH** turn for Banstead Heath.

7 Continue along the edge of **Banstead Heath** for 125m before turning ← onto a bridleway (wooden signpost) heading diagonally across the heath. At a ✖ keep ↑ (←) then fork → to follow the bridleway **SE** through the woods. Cross ↑ over the Dorking Road and continue on the bridleway, soon bearing → at a fork. Continue across the heath, keeping ↑ at ✖s – following the blue bridleway markers. At a ✖ with a signpost, continue ↑ (*Mogador*). Go through a couple of gates and continue across open fields to arrive at a ✖ of residential streets.

8 Take the second **RH** street (Buckland Road), which soon becomes a bridleway. At a ✖, continue ↑ along the edge of **Margery Wood** before crossing high above the M25 on a bridge. Continue ↑ to a gate, go through the gate and cross ↑ (**SE**) over the NDW, rejoining the GW. The path briefly leads along the lip of the escarpment before descending through a gate and continuing very steeply down to emerge on Underhill Park Road at the foot of **Colley Hill**. Continue ↑ onto Beech Road, bearing ← after 300m onto Brokes Road. At a T-junction turn → onto the A217 and arrive at **Reigate station** after 500m.

Approaching the steep south escarpment of the North Downs at Gangers Hill

9

Route 9
Warlingham–Biggin Hill loop

START/FINISH	Purley train station TQ 315 615
DISTANCE	38km (23½ miles)
ON ROAD	18km (11¼ miles)
OFF ROAD	20km (12¼ miles)
ASCENT	795m (2610ft)
GRADE	▲
TIME	3hrs 30mins–4hrs
MAPS	OS Explorer 146 and 147, Landranger 187
PUB	The White Bear, Fickleshole
CAFÉ	Café Papillon, Oxted

55% OFF ROAD

Overview

This route starts and finishes within the Borough of London, skirting the urban fringe and taking in an expansive loop through the east Surrey and west Kent countryside in between. Although nearly half the ride is on road, the roads in question are mostly the narrowest of country lanes, which link together the byways and bridleways accounting for the remainder of the route. The trail surfaces are generally good with mud and horse hoof-damage only really causing a problem in winter and during protracted periods of wet weather. West of the Surrey Hills, the terrain is noticeably less-wooded, with the exception of the southern slopes of the North Downs.

There are a few challenging climbs and rattling descents to contend with, not least the ascent of Gangers Hill and the preceding downhill along Pitchfont Lane on the steep southern escarpment of the North Downs' main ridge.

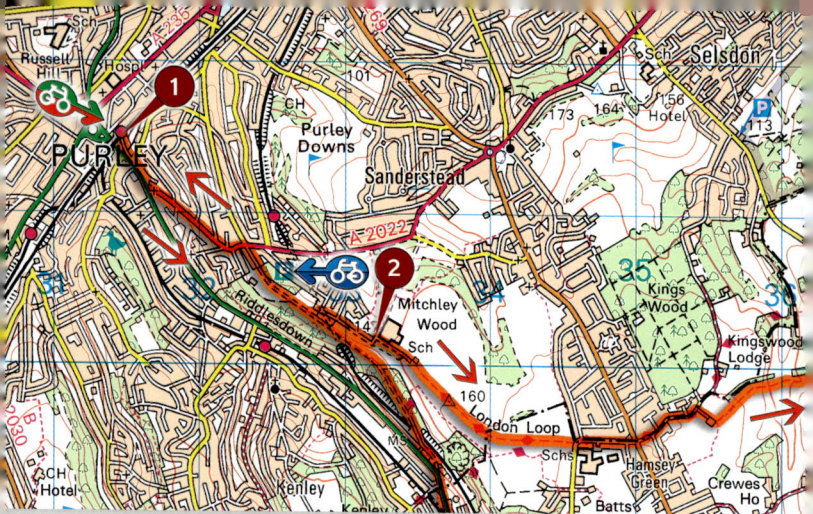

Directions

1 From **Purley station**, turn ← (SE) along the `A22` and go under the railway bridge. Take the first **LH** turn (*Selsdon* and *Sandserstead A2022*) and climb steadily along Downs Court Road. At a sharp bend, bear ← with the bend to continue along Mitchley Avenue. Take the next **RH** turn along Riddlesdown Road (no through road sign), continue ↑ through a wooden gate and follow the road to Riddlesdown car park at TQ 325 605, which is an alternative start/finish point if arriving by car. Continue ↑ along the chalk track, bearing ← at a fork then turning ← to go through a gate onto a residential road. Take the first → and continue along Honister Heights, turning ← onto Dunmail Drive at the end of the road.

2 Turn → onto a bridleway (*Public Bridleway Hamsey Green*) – part of **London Loop** (LDP) – before reaching the college campus. Follow the initially tree-lined path – muddy after wet weather – as it swings to the **left** and continue past a metal barrier onto a residential road. Continue ↑ along Tithepit Shaw Lane, keeping ↑ at a ✖ (dogleg → then ←) onto Kingswood Lane. Just before reaching the end of the road, which gives way to a track road (no through road sign), turn → onto Farleigh Common. Pass to the ← of stables, bear ← onto bridleway path (blue waymarker) and follow the often hoof-damaged track down and up again to arrive at Farleigh Road. Turn ← then turn → after 175m. Keep ↑ on the winding and ever-narrowing Farleigh Court Road for 2km. Watch out for a bridleway on the **left** (*Greenwich* and *New Addington NCN21*).

3 The tree-lined path soon descends steeply then climbs again; go through a bridlegate to join the road at **Fickleshole**. Turn ← and follow the road through the hamlet; just past Cox's Cottages, turn ← onto a tree-lined bridleway opposite Chelsham Court Farm (*Greenwich* and *New Addington NCN21*). Follow this disused road around to a ✗, cross ↑ (ignore NCN21, which turns left) over the road then bear → onto a bridleway that soon crosses a field and continue into Jewels Wood. Swing ← and keep ↑ to exit the woods onto the road at Jewels Hill.

Climbing along a snowy byway track near Biggin Hill

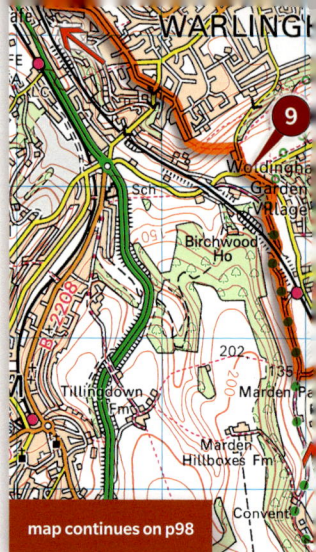

map continues on p98

Descend steeply with a sharp **LH** bend near the bottom, **taking care not to miss the first RH turn onto Oaklands Lane**. Follow this road for 650m before turning **→** onto a byway with a metal barrier. The track soon forks (green byway sign); bear **←** along the tree-lined byway, which rises almost imperceptibly for a while before climbing very steeply to reach a road at the top of the escarpment.

4 Turn **←** along Hesiers Road and follow it around to a **✗** – keep **↑** and continue for 750m before turning **←** onto a tree-lined bridleway. The bridleway descends steeply at length then shortly after bottoming out there is a short, very sharp climb that is virtually impossible in wet conditions. At the top of the climb the path turns sharply right before passing **Beddlestead Farm House** to arrive at a gate by a road. Go through, turn **→** and continue along Beddlestead Lane for 2km, climbing steadily before reaching a T-junction on **Titsey Hill**.

5 Turn **→** along the road (*Warlingham* and *Limpsfield*) and continue to a roundabout. Pass the first left-hand exit then come off the road and go through a gate to join a byway track. Descend very steeply with care along Pitchfont Lane – **check your speed as this track is popular with walkers and horse riders**.

6 The gradient eases as the track continues through Pitchfont Farm; keep **↑** as the byway becomes a tree-lined bridleway – can be churned up by farm vehicles – soon passing under the `M25` before reaching the `B269`. Turn **→** along the road for 500m and turn **→** again at a junction onto Bluehouse Lane (*Titsey* and *Croydon*); turn **←** after 300m onto Water Lane and keep **↑** for 1.3km, passing under a railway bridge before turning **→** at a junction onto Barrow Green Road, then immediately **←** (*cemetery*) onto Court Farm Lane. Watch out for a narrow bridleway path (blue marker) next to a cemetery gateway. Follow the bridleway across an arable field to arrive at a road by a T-junction. Turn **←** along Barrow Green Road for 800m.

7 Turn → onto a driveway (*Barrow Green Farm*). Follow the bridleway track between fences topped with razor wire and bristling with CCTV cameras – the frequently advertised guard dogs may also make you aware of their presence. Moving swiftly on, cross a bridge high above the M25 and bear ← along a bridleway track approaching the very steep south escarpment of the North Downs. Climb ever more steeply on a narrow, fenced path with a few roots for

added interest; you will be doing
well to get to the top of the climb
without getting (or falling) off and
pushing. In winter particularly
it can be impossible to ride this
bridleway in its upper reaches
due to hoof damage.

On the bridleway through Great Church Wood

8 At a ✗ with a signpost (*NDW/
Woldingham Countryside Walk*),
turn ← and climb steeply a
short way. Turn → onto a minor
road then after 250m turn ←
into a parking area; continue
↑ onto the bridleway path
through Great Church Wood,
descending a little then contouring along the escarpment, keeping ← at
a fork before descending steeply to a bridleway T-junction. Turn → and
contour along before descending into **Marden Park Farm**; turn ← through
the farmyard then turn → at a bridleway T-junction. Keep ↑ at a fork, pass
under the railway line then after 300m take the bridleway on the **right**
(*Greenwich* and *Warlingham NCN21*) through a copse to reach a minor road.
Turn ← along Woldingham Road (do not be tempted by the NCN21 sign
across the road) and continue to a ✗.

9 Keep ↑ (second →) onto Bug Hill (*Chelsham* and *Warlingham*), then after
150m turn ← onto a bridleway (no signpost) just past a house and climb
steeply at length up the escarpment. Emerge onto a residential road,
continue along Landscape Road, keep ↑ at a ✗ (still Landscape Road)
then shortly bear ← onto Westhall Road. Keep ↑ on this road for 1.2km,
descending to a T-junction. Turn ← and go under a bridge.

10 Turn → at a roundabout onto the `A22` (*London* and *Croydon*). Continue until,
just beyond a huge round gas tower, a bridleway known as Riddlesdown
Road climbs away from the **RH** side of the road in front of a builders'
merchant yard. Follow the track up and across a bridge over the railway line
and across the common, passing through Riddlesdown car park car park
(alternative finish) and back onto Mitchley Avenue. Retrace the outward
route to **Purley station**.

On the Pilgrim's Way ancient trackway (Route 12)

Routes around
Maidstone and the Medway Valley

Jungle biking on Oldbury Hill!

10

Route 10

Oldbury Hill and Mereworth Woods

START/FINISH	Borough Green train station TQ 609 574; or Oldbury Lane TQ 587 565
DISTANCE	27.5km (17 miles)
ON ROAD	9.75km (6 miles)
OFF ROAD	17.75km (11 miles)
ASCENT	550m (1805ft)
GRADE	▲
TIME	4hrs 30mins–5hrs
MAPS	OS Explorer 147 and 148, Landranger 188
PUB	The George and Dragon, Ightam; The Papermakers Arms, Plaxtol
CAFÉ	Café Troika, Borough Green; kiosk at weekends and holiday periods, Ightam Mote

Overview

This excellent ride takes in some very lovely countryside; from the jungle-crowned heights of Oldbury Hill to the forested expanse of Mereworth Woods, the route follows byways, bridleways and narrow country lanes through woodland, orchards, country house estates and picturesque Kentish villages. There are a couple of challenging climbs, some fine woodland singletrack and several tricky descents as well as a decent country pub or two – what else could you possibly want from a ride?

Directions

1 From **Borough Green station** turn → on the `A227`, forking ← onto the High Street after 100m. Keep ↑ over a ✖ with the `A25`, then stay ↑ past a junction continuing onto Quarry Hill Road. Keep ↑ at a roundabout to continue (Quarry Hill Road) along a sunken lane through a quarry. At a fork, bear → onto Thong Lane and continue to a dogleg ✖. Turn → and continue along Mill Lane for 1km before reaching a T-junction and turning → onto the `A227`. Take the first ← onto Sevenoaks Road by a half-timbered house (*Seal* and *Sevenoaks*) then take the second **RH** turn (↑) to cross both carriageways of the `A25` and continue ↑ along Oldbury Lane.

2 After 500m, at a sharp bend keep ↑ on Oldbury Lane (no through road sign), which becomes a bridleway.

Alternative start/finish at Oldbury Lane

A If arriving by car, you can start and finish the ride here; park considerately on the lane making sure other traffic can get past your vehicle.

Keep ↑ at a fork, climbing steadily; pass to the right of a garage onto a narrow path (stone Public Bridleway marker). Begin climbing steeply into

Spring greenery in Fish Ponds Wood

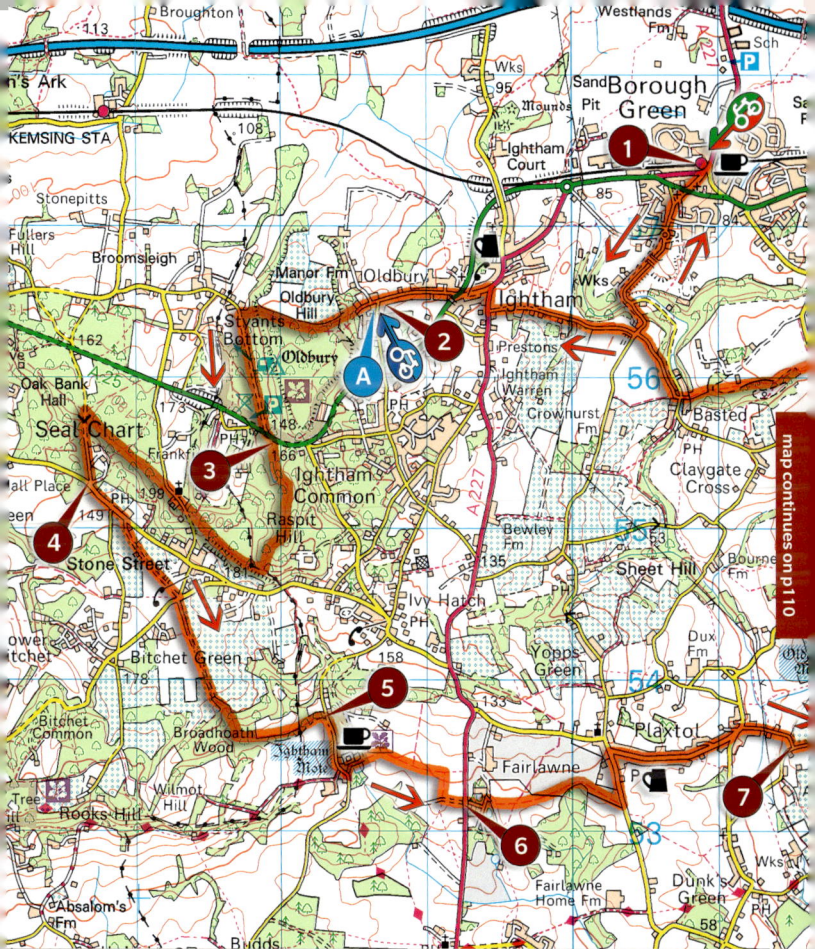

woodland on a sunken lane – a series of wooden anti-erosion steps adds to the fun! Continue climbing along an eroded sandstone path – near impossible in wet conditions – reaching a path ✖ at the top of the climb. Continue ⬆ on a byway (no sign) ignoring the signposted bridleway on the left. At a ✖ by an **Oldbury Hill** signboard, bear ➡ and continue downhill, keeping ➡ as you descend. At the bottom of the descent turn ⬅ onto Styants Bottom Road. Arrive at a T-junction with the busy A25 after 900m;

dogleg ← then → across the road (with care) onto a bridleway (green bridleway sign) leading through woodland.

3 Continue through Fish Ponds Wood along the sandy woodland track, passing several ponds, eventually arriving below an embankment at the foot of some very large steps; a narrow path to the right of the steps snakes up the slope. At the top, turn → onto a bridleway and continue along a firm track (muddy after rain) for 650m, ignoring intersecting paths. Emerge onto a minor road and keep ↑ (→), passing a school and a **church**, then at a **RH** bend bear ← to join a bridleway (green bridleway sign) leading into **Redhill Wood**. The main path can be hoof-damaged – especially after wet weather – but some excellent singletrack paths can be followed just to the left. Continue ↑ for 750m to arrive at a minor road, turn ← downhill along the sunken lane.

4 At a T-junction with Stone Street Road (Give Way sign) turn ← and then stay left at a fork shortly after. Turn → opposite the **Padwell Arms** pub onto a gravel track (bridleway sign may be engulfed by hedge). Continue through orchards then at a road ✗ continue ↑ along a narrow initially tarmac lane (green bridleway sign). Keep ↑ past orchards; where the main track swings sharply right near the treeline, continue ↑ on a narrower path descending through woods (steps to negotiate), swinging sharp ← before the gradient eases and the track soon emerges on Mote Road.

5 Turn → and continue with the grounds of **Ightam Mote manor house** on your left for 400m, passing several venerable houses before turning sharp ← between red brick gate pillars (*Ightam Mote*, blue arrow bridleway markers). Bear → past the manor house and continue past the car park and keep ↑ onto the bridleway track between fields. Follow the bridleway between hedgerows as it bears **right** then continue through a gate into a field, turn → (blue waymarker arrow) along the tree-lined field edge, go through a bridlegate then turn ← along a track road to arrive at a T-junction.

6 Cross ↑ over the busy **A227** (take care) and go through a bridlegate (blue arrow) into **Fairlawne Estate**. Continue to a T-junction, turn ← then shortly → following bridlepath signs to enter a field through a bridlegate. Follow the grassy path through the wooded estate grounds; keep ↑ at a path ✗, go through a gateway in a stock fence then bear → along a tree-lined avenue, soon passing through a metal estate gate to arrive at a T-junction with School Lane. Turn ← along the road then after 300m turn → along The Street;

Singletrack trail in Redhill Wood

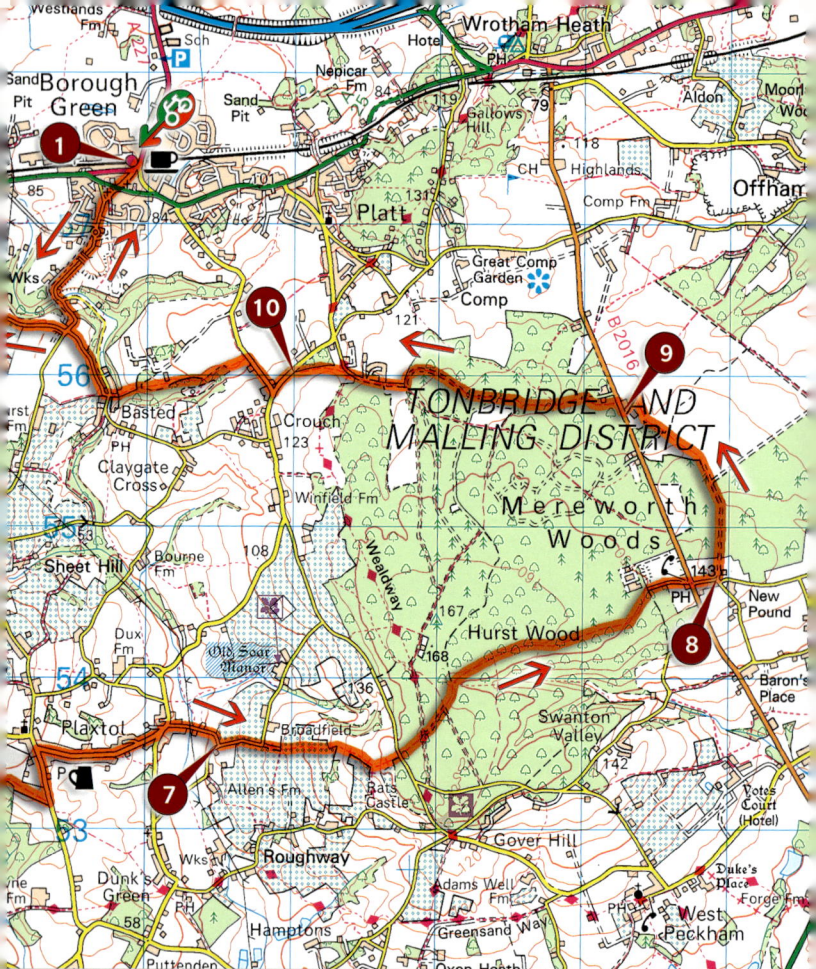

continue downhill through **Plaxtol** passing the **Papermakers Arms**; ignore a right-hand turn to Dunk Green by a red telephone box, turn ➜ along Brook Lane (*Old Soar Manor*).

7 At the T-junction with Allens Lane, turn ← (becomes Old Soar Road) and continue for 300m to where the road turns sharp left and keep ↑ (➜) onto a tree-lined byway track by a wall (green byway signpost). Continue along the byway, ignoring a track on the right and climb at length on a steady gradient as the track narrows. At a track T-junction bear ← to continue uphill and soon emerge at a minor road; continue ↑ onto a bridleway (green bridleway sign) opposite. Continue ↑ on the main path contouring along through magnificent woodland, ignoring intersecting paths – keep → at a fork with a metal barrier gate. After 2.3km, arrive at the busy **B2016** next to The Beeches restaurant. Cross ↑ (with care) onto Beech Road.

8 After 150m, opposite New Pound Lane, turn ← between hedges onto a (unsignposted) tree-lined bridleway. Continue into woodland and keep ↑ over two ✗ s – the bridleway can be very churned up by forestry work. At the next path junction bear ← (↑) as the main track swings right. After 400m turn sharp ← by twin telegraph poles with a transformer onto a narrow track, soon passing the red-brick Longwall House.

9 Emerge at the **B2016**, turn → then ← after 20m onto a narrow path entering woodland (green bridleway sign). Follow the earth track next to a fence around boarding kennels then bear ← away from the fence onto a more distinct track (faded bridleway marker). Continue along the bridleway, which joins a wide forestry road, then bear → at a fork. Continue ↑ on a gentle descent before swinging ←. Where the track swings right again, turn sharply → to go through a wooden bridlegate then descend a little along a bridleway, passing a luxury housing estate and joining tarmac opposite a street sign for *The Old Saw Mill*. Take the second turn ← (first left is a byway) onto a narrow track with a concrete Public Bridleway marker.

10 At a junction with a minor road, turn ← then → at the next junction onto Crouch Lane. At the bottom of a dip just past the driveway of Sotts Hole Cottage go down several wooden steps to join a (unsignposted) bridleway through woods. Climb a little, briefly descend steeply, then continue on a narrow path next to a paddock (can be overgrown in summer) joining tarmac before arriving at a T-junction with Basted Lane. Dogleg ← then → onto Mill Lane (note: this is incorrectly marked as Basted Lane on some OS maps). Continue along Mill Lane to a ✗, turn → along Thong Lane and retrace your outward route to **Borough Green station**.

It's a slippery slope on Wise's Lane

11

Route 11

Meopham–Wrotham loop

START/FINISH	Meopham train station TQ 641 679; or Meopham Green TQ 641 651
DISTANCE	38.75km (24 miles)
ON ROAD	15.25km (9½ miles)
OFF ROAD	23.5km (14½ miles)
ASCENT	755m (2475ft)
GRADE	▲
TIME	4hrs 30mins–5hrs
MAPS	OS Explorer 147 and 148, Landranger 188
PUB	Amazon and Tiger, Harvel; Anchor and Hope, near Ash
CAFÉ	The Bluebell Café, Trosley Country Park, Vigo Village

60% OFF ROAD

Overview

At times the loop of wooded byways, lanes and bridle-ways that make up much of this route give the impression that you are riding along one

long green tunnel – quite a feat in such a densely populated part of the country. However, just in case this sounds like a pleasant and relaxing pedal along country lanes, it should be noted that this a long, demanding route with a number of climbs, several of which are very tough.

The route loops around the gently rolling countryside to the west of the Medway Valley and is bounded to the east and south by the M20, save for one brief excursion to the south of the motorway. The steep south escarpment of the North Downs, just north of the M20, provides the venue for several of this route's more challenging ascents and descents.

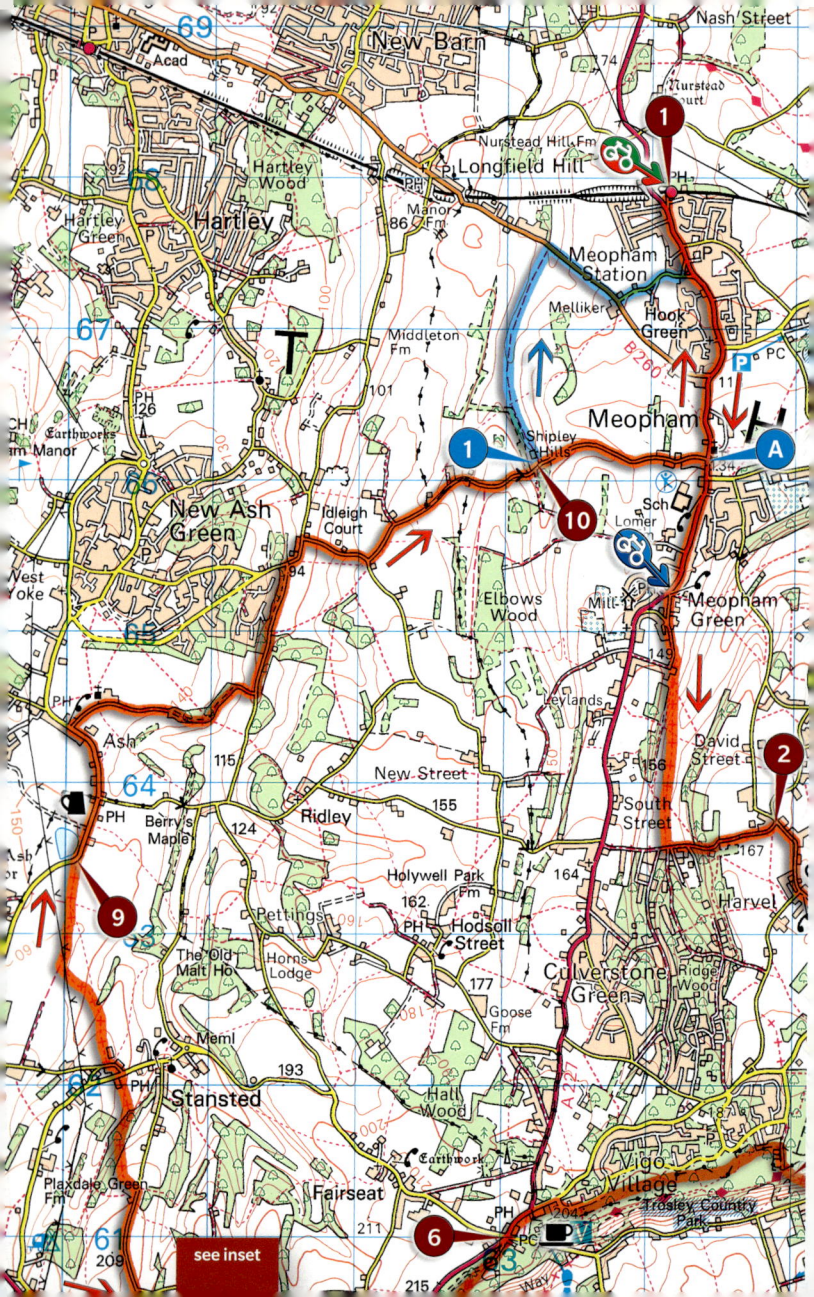

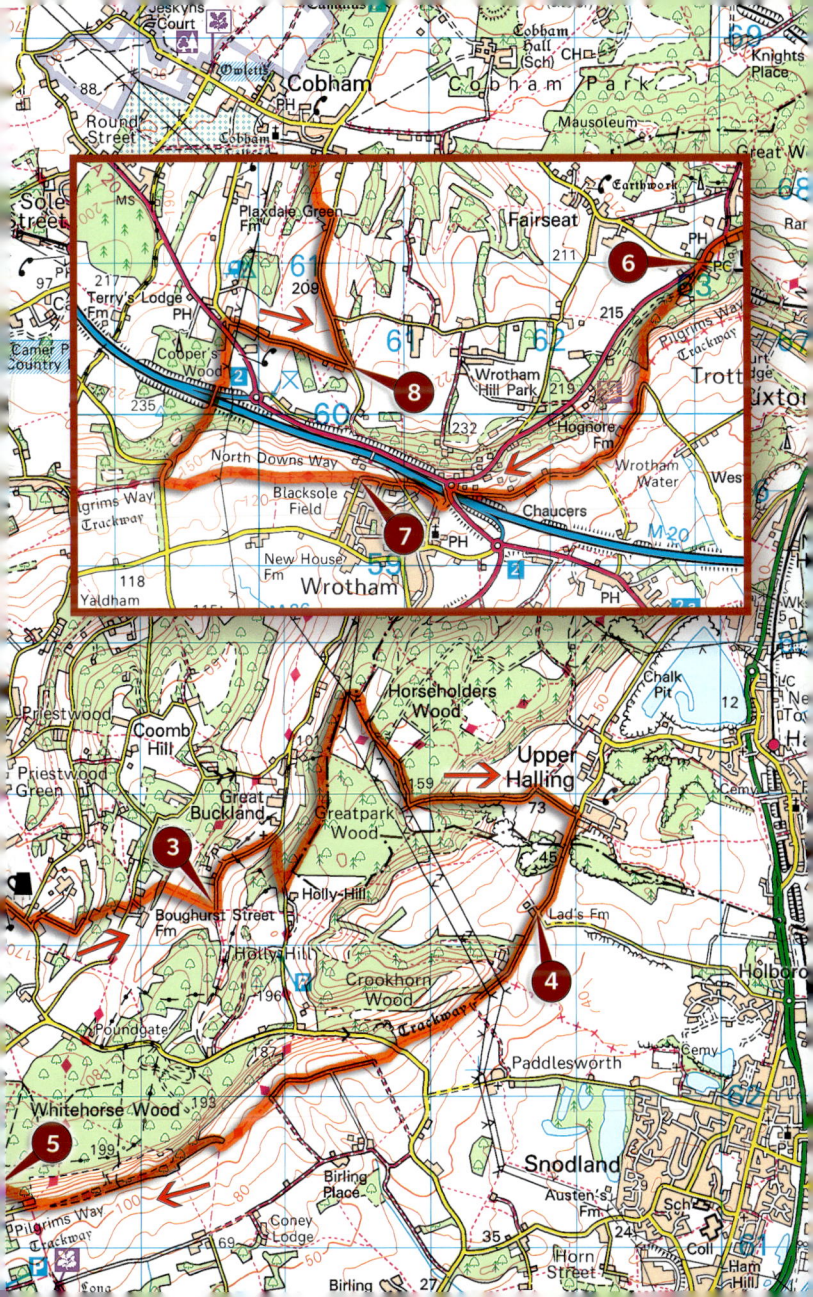

Descending a bridleway towards Wrangling Lane

Directions

1 From **Meopham station** continue ↑ onto the `A227` Wrotham Road and stay with it for 2.8km before turning ← onto Steele's Lane by the war memorial at **Meopham Green** (alternative start/finish point – park considerately by the green). Continue past the village green and onto a byway track (green byway sign) with a signpost reading *Unsuitable for Motor Vehicles*. Continue along a tree-lined track, dogleg ← then → at a path T-junction, descend and follow the byway ↑ for 1.2km, climbing a little before reaching a ✖. Turn ← (green byway sign), descend a little along Heron Hill Lane and continue ↑ (←) on the byway (red waymarker arrows) where the main track bends right. Climb steeply through woods – slippery when wet – then follow the track around to a T-junction.

2 Turn → along Whitehill Road and continue through **Harvel**, bearing ← (↑) past the **Amazon and Tiger** pub. Pass a left-hand turn and continue past a small green with a village signpost then turn ← onto a farm road (green bridleway signpost). After 120m turn → off the farm road onto a bridleway path. The path bends sharply **left** then **right**, continuing by Little Delmar

Farm before emerging on a minor road. Turn ← a short way then turn →
onto a path (green bridleway signpost) between two driveways. Turn ←
at a path T-junction and continue to a path junction with the Weald Way
footpath (continuing ↑); bear → and descend along a field edge to arrive at
a T-junction.

3 Turn ← onto Wrangling Lane byway track and continue along the hedge-
lined track, which soon gives way to tarmac; after 750m turn sharply →
onto a track road (green byway signpost), which soon becomes rough and
climb very steeply up a wooded hillside. At the top of the climb, turn sharp
← to join the NDW along another byway track. Cruise along the top of the
escarpment for 1.5km (the NDW turns right as a footpath after 1km) on
the stone-chipped track before reaching a T-junction. Turn → onto another
byway track, which bends sharp left after 850m and descends along Chapel
Lane, which bends sharp right at a road/path ✗ after the same distance.

4 At the ✗ at **Upper Halling**, turn → along the PW. Where the road bends
sharp left by **Lad's Farm** after 700m, keep ↑ onto an initially surfaced track
road (green restricted byway signpost). Continue ↑ climbing gently along
the firm byway track, keeping ← (↑) to go around a barrier at a fork and
crossing ↑ over a minor road after 1.4km. Contour along the pleasant
tree-lined track and after a further 1km the byway rejoins the NDW; where
a byway track climbs to the right, keep ↑ to stay on the NDW bridleway.
After 1.2 km the NDW crosses the WW and emerges onto tarmac by several
houses. Turn → here (signpost with red byway marker) and climb steeply
up the wooded south escarpment of the North Downs; the path has a series
of wooden anti-erosion steps making the steep climb challenging in dry
conditions and near impossible in the wet.

5 At the top of the climb the NDW turns left becoming a footpath; continue
↑ on the byway for another 100m before turning ← through a gate onto
an ancient trackway leading through Great Wood in **Trosley Country Park**.
Stay ↑ on the main track for almost 1.5km – give way to other users –
before turning → where an access road leads into the park. Turn ← along a
residential road and continue to a T-junction; turn ← along Harvel Road for
250m then bear ← along the `A227` for a further 250m, passing **The Vigo Inn**
and reaching a ✗.

6 At the ✗ turn ← just past a brick bus shelter onto the NDW, which is a byway
at this point (green *NDW* sign). Descend very steeply along this track, which

has plenty of wooden anti-erosion steps for added entertainment, and emerge at a bend on a minor road; keep ➔ and continue ↑ for 1.75km climbing steadily along the winding road to arrive at a busy roundabout. Hop onto the path on the **LH** side of the road and take the first ← turn off the roundabout along the `A20`. Where the path runs out, cross ↑

On the North Downs Way near Vigo Village

over the road (with great care) to rejoin the NDW/PW (*LDP* signpost). Follow a path to a bend in a road, bear ← for 150m then turn ➔ along Old London Road for 350m. Turn ← onto the **PW** (brown *NDW* signpost). Continue along the narrow lane and keep ↑ along the byway (green byway sign) where the road turns sharp left.

7 Keep ↑ along the excellent byway track for 1.4km. Arrive at a T-junction and turn ➔ onto Exedown Road, climb for a short way before leaving the road at a bend, pass around a gate to join a bridleway path (green bridleway sign). Climb very steeply up the escarpment on the stone-chipped path, then cross the `M20` on a footbridge. Go through a metal gate and follow the bridleway past trees along a paddock edge; go through an old metal gate and soon emerge at the `A20` (**this is a fast road so take care**); turn ← then take the first **RH** turn (*Stansted Village*, *Fairseat*, *Ridley*) then turn ➔ onto Labour-In-Vain Road. Continue ↑ along the narrowing road for 900m.

8 At the T-junction, turn sharp ← onto Tumblefield Road. Continue ↑ for 1km, descending, climbing then descending again before turning ← onto a byway (green byway signpost may be overgrown) at Stansted Lodge Farm – **this is easily missed if you're travelling at speed**. Head straight through the farmyard onto the tree-lined byway track; descend steeply through woods on the rough track, which bottoms out and climbs gently before emerging onto Plaxdale Green Road at **Stansted**. Dogleg ➔ then turn ← along

Hatham Green Lane and follow this round a bend, turning → and passing a gated driveway to join another tree-lined byway track known as Wise's Lane (green byway signpost). Descend then climb a little; bear → (↑) at a path junction to stay on the byway and continue along this lovely track, soon emerging at a bend in a road.

9 Join the road, bearing → (↑) to continue along South Ash Road. After 1km, turn → along Church Road by a weather-boarded house. Continue along the lane passing by the grand house at Ash Place Farm, joining a byway track where the road runs out and soon descending through woods to arrive at a minor road. Turn ← and continue for 1km to a T-junction, turn → (*Longfield Hill*) then take the next → turn to climb along Idleigh Court Road. At the top of the climb, bear ← (*Meopham*) and continue for 1.5km, descending, climbing then descending to **Shipley Hills**.

Variant route to Meopham station

1 If you fancy a challenge, turn ← through a gate onto a bridleway path (green bridleway signpost) passing a collection of barns and continuing along Gorse Bottom. Keep ↑ along the valley floor where the path cuts across very bumpy arable fields to arrive at a minor road after 1.5km. Turn → on the **B260** – you're probably best staying on the pavement alongside this fast section of road – and climb gently for 600m before turning ← onto Melliker Lane (*Hook Green*). Continue ↑ for 500m before turning ← by a small green and continuing to a junction with the **A227**. Turn ← and retrace your outward route to **Meopham station**.

10 Continue along the road, climbing steadily before levelling out and continuing to a T-junction with the **A227**. Turn ← and retrace your outward route to **Meopham station**.

Alternative finish at Meopham Green

A Turn → at the T-junction with the **A227** and continue ↑ for 1km before turning ← by Meopham Green war memorial.

Muddy byway on the North Downs Way near Kit's Coty

12

Route 12

Bearsted, Detling Hill and Blue Bell Hill

START/FINISH	Bearsted train station TQ 799 561; or Hucking car park TQ 848 581
DISTANCE	47.5km (29 miles); or 33.5km (21 miles)
ON ROAD	22km (13 miles); or 16km (10 miles)
OFF ROAD	25.5km (16 miles); or 17.5km (11 miles)
ASCENT	925m (3035ft); or 620m (2035ft)
GRADE	▲
TIME	4hrs 30mins–5hrs 30mins; or 3hrs–4hrs
MAPS	OS Explorer 148, Landranger 188
PUB	The Robin Hood at Burham
CAFÉ	Mikey's Diner, Old Chatham Road, Blue Bell Hill

55%
OFF ROAD

Overview

This is a real cross-country route that puts the miles in along a swathe of the North Downs to the north and east of Maidstone and the Medway Valley, for the most part following a variety of bridleways, byways and narrow country lanes. The terrain is generally firm: the challenge comes with the multiple climbs and descents of the North Downs' steep southern escarpment. The route never strays too far from north Kent's urban centres and criss-crosses the Eurostar railway line, the M20 and several arterial roads to boot; nonetheless civilisation is quickly left

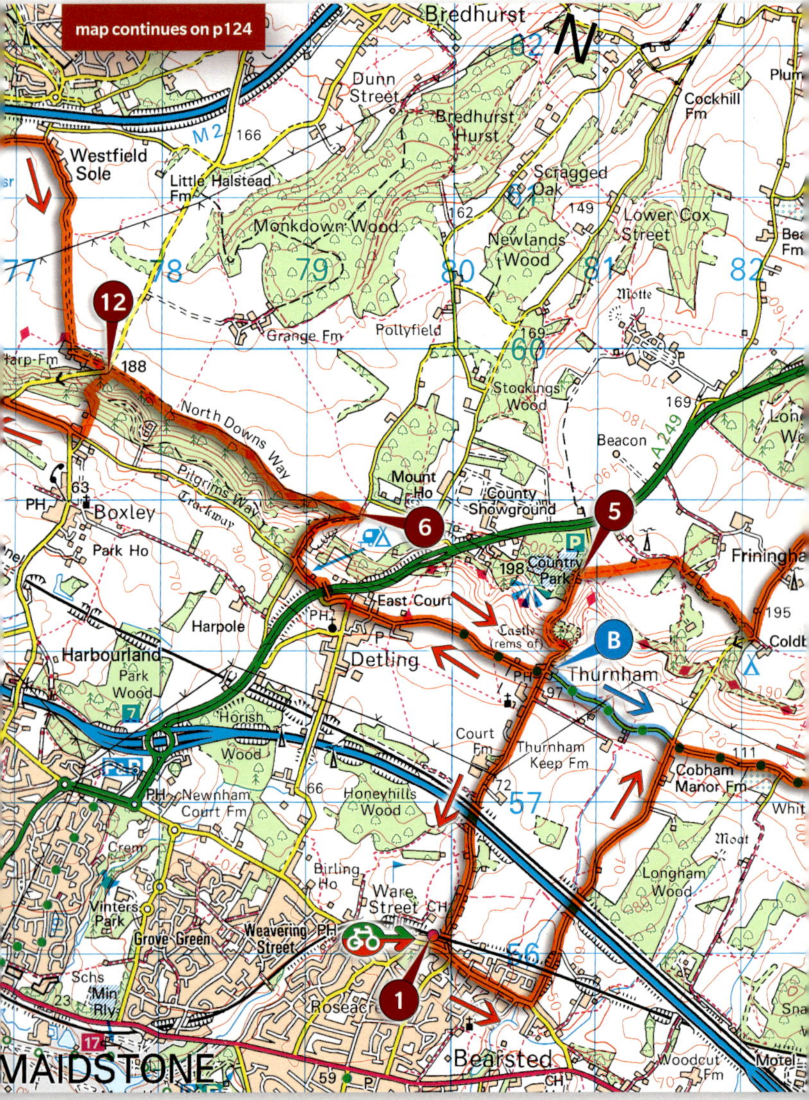

map continues on p124

N

Bredhurst

Dunn
Street

Cockhill
Fm

Plum

Bredhurst
Hurst

Westfield
Sole

166

Little Halstead
Fm

Scragged
Oak

149

Lower Cox
Street

Bea
Fm

Monkdown Wood

18   79   80   81   82

Newlands
Wood

Motte

77

188

Grange Fm

Pollyfield

60

169

169

Lon
We

Harp Fm

North Downs Way

Stockings
Wood

Beacon

A 249

Pilgrims Way

Mount
Ho

County
Showground

63

Trackway

6

Friningha

Boxley

Park Ho

PH

5

198 Country
Park

195

East Court

B

Coldt

Harpole

PH

Detling

Thurnham

190

Harbourland

Park
Wood

Court
Fm

Thurnham
Keep Fm

197

111

Horish
Wood

57

Cobham
Manor Fm

Whit

PH Newnham
Court Fm

66

Honeyhills
Wood

72

Moat

Crem

Vinters
Park

Birling
Ho

Longham
Wood

Grove Green

Weavering
Street

Ware
Street CH

56

1

Schs
Min
Rly

Roseac

Bearsted

Woodcut
Fm

Motel

MAIDSTONE

17

59

CH

Sna

behind when you're out along the wooded escarpments. There are some great views across the Medway Valley to enjoy when you take a breather.

As the route is long and narrow and there are many criss-crossing byways, bridleways and lanes, there is plenty of scope for shortening the ride if you wish. See the map and route descriptions for a couple of options.

Directions

1 From **Bearsted station**, turn ← onto Ware Street (becomes The Street) and continue ↑ for 750m before turning ← onto Water Lane by a large house (brown *Countryside Walks and Rides* signpost). Go through a tunnel, pass beneath the **M20** then the **Eurostar railway line** and climb steadily along the lane to arrive at a ✖. Turn → along the **PW** (*Hollingbourne*) and continue for 1.7km to **Broad Street**.

2 Pass through Broad Street and after 1km turn ← onto a byway (green byway signpost) next to large agricultural sheds. Continue along the farm road, which passes next to a house and becomes a tree-lined earth track as it begins to climb steeply up the south escarpment of the North Downs. The track becomes steeper and crosses the NDW near the top of the climb, continuing through woodland.

3 Beyond the top of the climb, keep ↑ on the byway track as it begins gently descending through Bolton's Wood. Look out for a Woodland

Trust marker post on your right, turn ← here towards a wooden gate then dogleg → onto a bridleway path (blue arrow waymarker) – hoof-damage can be a problem in winter. After 400m the track swings sharply **left** then comes to a T-junction by an elaborate wooden gate 200m further on. Turn → and keep ↑ along the grassy bridleway, soon joining a metalled track; continue around a gate to arrive on a minor road next to a flint-walled church.

Alternative start at Hucking car park

A Turn ← (soon passing the flint-walled church) and continue ↑ through **Hucking**. Follow the route description in paragraph **4**.

4 Turn ← and continue through **Hucking**, descending steeply then climbing before turning → after 1km just past **The Hook and Hatchet** pub. Continue along the lane for 750m before turning sharp ← onto the single-track Coldblow Lane. At a fork bear → to soon pass **Little Budd's Farm** and snake along the lane past a couple of communications towers. Just before a left-hand turning to Coldblow Farm, turn → into woods along a bridleway (green bridleway signpost). Follow the path through the woods, passing the grounds of Friningham Manor before jinking ← then → onto a farm road. Continue past a copse, then just opposite a Wireless Transmitting Station fork ← off the track onto a bridleway (probably no signpost) and head diagonally **WSW** across an arable field (the path may be obscured by crops).

5 On reaching a minor road (Castle Hill) by **White Horse Wood Country Park**, turn ← and continue along the lane, soon descending steeply. **Slow down** on entering **Thurnham** and turn → at a ✗ (*Detling* and *Maidstone*) by the **Black Horse Inn**. Continue along the **PW** arriving in **Detling** after 1.5km. At a T-junction opposite **The Cock Horse** pub, turn → then immediately ← soon turning → off the road onto a ramped pedestrian bridge (*NDW*) over the `A249`. Once across turn → along the PW; just past a left-hand turn (Harple Lane) bear → onto the **NDW** (wooden *NDW* signpost with a red byway marker) and climb steeply along the narrow, initially tarmac lane, passing a quarry.

6 At the top of the climb the byway swings **left**. Watch out for a waymarker post and turn ← (blue arrow NDW bridleway marker) along the top of the wooded escarpment following the rolling bridleway track for 2km. Where

National Cycle Route Millennium Milepost near the A229

the NDW jinks right off the main track, continue ↑ to descend steeply through Boxley Wood, then swing ← before emerging at a road junction by Downs View Farm. Turn → onto the second (lower) of two narrow parallel roads and continue along the **PW**. At a T-junction turn → (↑) and continue for 500m; at a sharp right bend continue ↑ to leave the road, passing round a green metal gate and continuing along a tree-lined permissive bridleway track road, which rises and falls beneath the steep escarpment, soon joining the PW on a byway track.

7 Descend and cross a bridge over the **Eurostar railway line**; fork → past a motor home dealers then take the second → past a service station (NCN Millennium Milepost and *NDW* signpost) and pass under the **A229** through a subway.

Shorter route variant

1 The route can be shortened here by forking → at the Millennium Milepost onto a byway track and climbing steadily above the **Eurostar railway tunnel**.

At a ✖, turn ➔ onto Lower Warren Road and follow the route description from paragraph **11**. Using this alternative would reduce the route time to 3–4hrs, and the distance to 33.5km (21 miles).

Turn ← then ➔ after 75m onto a tree-lined byway track (NDW); follow the track, which passes nearby Kit's Coty ancient burial chambers, and emerge at a road junction. Cross ↑ (with care) to join the **LH** carriageway (*Eccles* and *Burham*). Follow the PW/Rochester Road for 1.7km and opposite a left-hand turn onto Court Road, turn ➔ off the road onto a byway track next to a bus stop (green byway signpost). Climb steadily and after 1km the gradient becomes very steep – this is a long, tough climb.

8 At the top of the climb turn ← onto Common Road along the NDW.

Shorter route variant

To effect a short cut at the top of the climb, turn ➔ along Common Road and follow the route description from paragraph **10**, which would reduce the distance to 39km (24½ miles) and knock 30mins off the time.

The road runs out by **Burham Hill Farm**; continue ↑ onto a farm track, which soon becomes a byway known as Hill Road. The track descends with gathering momentum, where it swings sharply left, keep ↑ on the **NDW** (possibly no signpost) on a narrower bridleway path. The chalk track levels as views open up across The Medway and its bridges, before descending again, passing through a gate, crossing over the **Eurostar railway line** and bottoming out through **Nashenden Farm**.

9 Turn sharp ➔ to part company with the NDW (blue bridleway signpost) and continue along the initially tarmac lane running parallel to the **M2**. Pass around a gate where tarmac gives way to gravel track; at a fork, bear ← to continue on the bridleway, which eventually emerges onto another road. Turn ➔ to cross a bridge over the **Eurostar railway line** and follow the road around to the dead end by Upper Nashenden Farm. Turn ➔ and then bear ← briefly onto a track, then immediately fork ➔ onto a bridleway path and begin the long steady climb through woodland back to the top of the ridge. Pass **The Robin Hood** pub before re-emerging on Common Road after 1.7km. Turn ←.

10 Continue along Common Road, crossing over the `A229` after 1.3km. At a ✖ in **Blue Bell Hill Village**, cross ↑ to continue along Mill Lane. The road swings sharply **right** and becomes Warren Road; continue along this narrow old Roman Road for 1.5km – descending steeply before arriving at a T-junction.

11 Turn ← onto Lower Warren Road and continue along the lane, passing a few houses before the road gives way to a byway track, which climbs ever more steeply up through Frith Wood along a flinty track before levelling out and exiting the woodland. Arriving at a T-junction on a sharp bend, turn → (↑) and follow the narrow Bell Lane for over 1km, before turning → at a T-junction. Continue along Harp Farm Road for 1.75km to arrive at a T-junction; continue ↑ onto a bridleway (**NDW**), passing around a gate.

12 Retrace your outward route along the top of the escarpment, turning → at the path junction to descend steeply along a byway track (NDW). On reaching the road, turn ← along the **PW**, continue to the junction with the `A249` and recross the pedestrian bridge. Once over, turn ← then at the T-junction dogleg → then ← to continue through **Detling** to arrive at a ✖ in **Thurnham**.

Alternative finish at Hucking car park

B Continue ↑ at the ✖ in **Thurnham** (*Hollingbourne*) for 2.75km to **Broad Street**. Follow the route description in paragraph **2** to reach the flint-walled church in **Hucking**. Turn → and soon → again to return to the **car park**.

Turn → past the **Black Horse Inn** and descend steadily along Thurnham Lane. Pass under the **Eurostar railway line** and the `M20`. After another 800m, pass under a railway bridge and continue to a T-junction, turn → to arrive back at **Bearsted station**.

Climbing steeply on West Down (Route 14)

Routes around Ashford

Fighting through the mud near Faggs Wood

13

Route 13

Bilsington and Faggs Wood loop

Start/Finish	Hamstreet train station TR 001 337
Distance	25.75km (16 miles)
On road	10.5km (6½ miles)
Off road	15.25km (9½ miles)
Ascent	200m (655ft)
Grade	■
Time	2hrs 30mins–3hrs 30mins
Maps	OS Explorer 137, Landranger 179 and 189
Pub	The Duke's Head, Hamstreet; The King's Head, Shadoxhurst
Café	The Coffee Shop, Hamstreet

60% OFF ROAD

Overview

This route is actually some way south of the North Downs in the low country, south of Ashford. As a result the ride is without the big climbs and rattling descents characteristic of the downland ridges and escarpments – making it probably the easiest ride in this guidebook. However, this route merits inclusion here because of the number of byway tracks it links up and also because Faggs Wood provides plenty of scope for exploration. The ride is something of a doddle in dry weather, but beware – after periods of rain some of the trails can be a total quagmire!

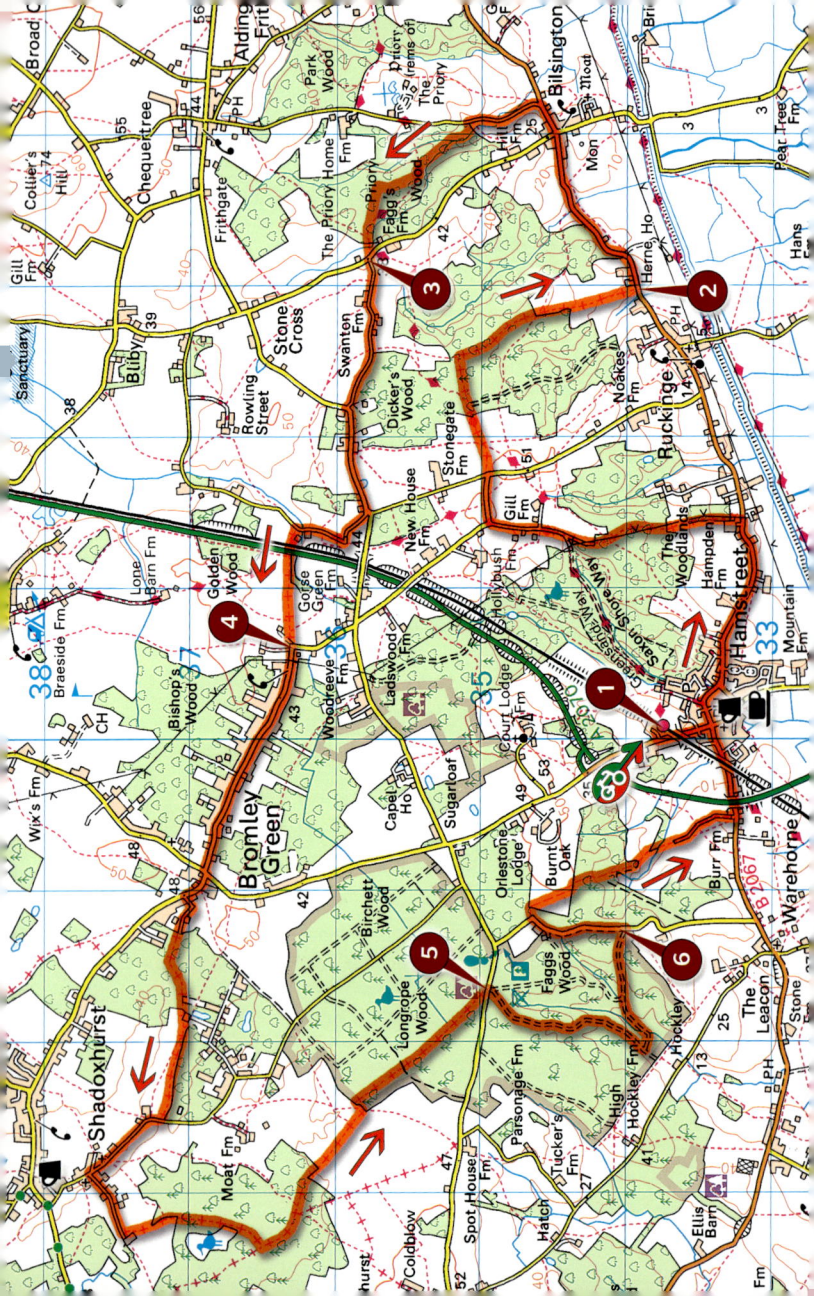

Directions

1 From **Hamstreet station** car park, turn ← onto the `B2067`, passing under the railway line before coming to a ✕. Turn ← (*Ruckinge*) and continue along the road for 1.5km before turning ← onto a tree-lined byway track (can be rutted by farm vehicles). The earth track continues through Barrow Wood becoming a tarmac lane as it passes through **Gill Farm**. At a fork, turn → along the lane and continue to a ✕ – keep ↑ onto another tree-lined byway track. Stay with the byway track as it turns sharply **right** to continue for a further 1.4km before emerging on the `B2067` once more.

2 Turn ← and keep ↑ over the ✕ at **Bilsington** then take the first **LH** turn along Priory Road; after 500m turn ← onto an unmarked track – next to a signposted footpath – leading into **Priory Wood** and bear →. Follow the track through the woods, initially next to a stream; the track is briefly intersected by a footpath – the Saxon Shore Way (SSW), go over a footbridge where the footpath forks left then bear → along the track. The track

Following the stream through Priory Wood

Over or under? Fallen tree in Priory Wood

eventually bends sharp **left** then shortly arrives at a minor road just north of **Fagg's Farm**.

3 Turn → then dogleg ← onto Swanton Lane; at a T-junction bear ← (↑) and continue to a ✘. Turn → along Brisley Lane. Follow the lane around for 600m then turn ← (signposted bridleway), passing stables to arrive at a gated level crossing. Cross when safe to do so, then cross the `A2070` with care. Continue ↑ along a tree-lined byway track (deeply rutted by 4WDs and often waterlogged). The byway emerges onto Bromley Green Road at a bend.

4 Continue ↑ (→) along this road for 1.7km to reach a ✘. Continue ↑ (*Shadoxhurst*) onto Hornash Lane. After 250m, turn ← onto a byway (green byway sign). Follow the byway all the way until it emerges on Church Lane. Turn → and follow the lane until you come to a ✘ in **Shadoxhurst**. Turn ← and continue along Duck Lane to Glebe Farm. Bear ← here onto the byway track and follow it around to the next track junction. Bear ← and follow the bridleway track ↑. At a fork, bear ← and continue ↑. After 1km dogleg ← then → and continue ↑ again for 1.2km before emerging on Birchett Lane.

5 Cross ↑ to go through the Forestry Commission gate into **Faggs Wood** – there are lots of trails to explore in this wood if you have the time and energy; some are quite technical and **there are some fast downhills, so approach with caution**! Take the **RH** track and continue steadily downhill until the descent bottoms out where there is a confluence of trails. Take the **LH** track and continue ↑ uphill; the path narrows before emerging onto a road.

6 Turn ← onto Malthouse Lane and continue along the road for 650m until you come to a bridleway on the **RH** side at a bend. Follow the rutted bridleway through a gate into a meadow (blue marker). Continue diagonally, bearing → across the meadow and making for a gate on the far side. Go through the gate, bear ← and continue through woods to another gate. Go through into another meadow, keep ← (↑) and make for a large metal stock gate. Go through, then at a left-hand bend keep ↑ on a narrow path until it emerges on the `B2067`. Turn ← out on the road and continue under the `A2070` then under the railway line before reaching a ✘ in **Hamstreet**. Turn ← (passing under the railway once more) before arriving back at **Hamstreet station**.

Winding byway track near Pett Street Farm

Route 14

Wye Downs loop

Start/Finish	Wye train station **TR 048 470**
Distance	21.5km (13¾ miles)
On road	6.5km (4½ miles)
Off road	15km (9¼ miles)
Ascent	510m (1675ft)
Grade	▲
Time	2hrs 30mins–3hrs
Maps	OS Explorer 137 and 138, Landranger 189 and 190
Pub	The Tickled Trout, Wye
Café	Crown Coffee, Wye

14

70% OFF ROAD

Overview

This route starts and finishes in the historic and picturesque village of Wye, nestled beneath the downland ridge bearing its name. Byways, bridleways and quiet country lanes are linked together to create a fine ride through some very lovely countryside. The NDW puts in several appearances along the way, so you'll likely encounter the odd walker tackling the LDP as well as the occasional horse and rider. Although this route takes in an area relatively close to Ashford and Canterbury, it is nonetheless surprisingly quiet.

Although this route is relatively short it should not be underestimated. After periods of wet weather it can be very muddy in parts and the less-frequented areas can be overgrown in summer; many of the signposts and waymarkers along the route can also become obscured. There are a few tough climbs and tricky descents to keep you on your toes, but in between you can enjoy the peaceful atmosphere and expansive views across the Garden of England.

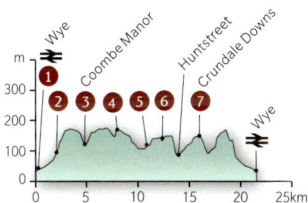

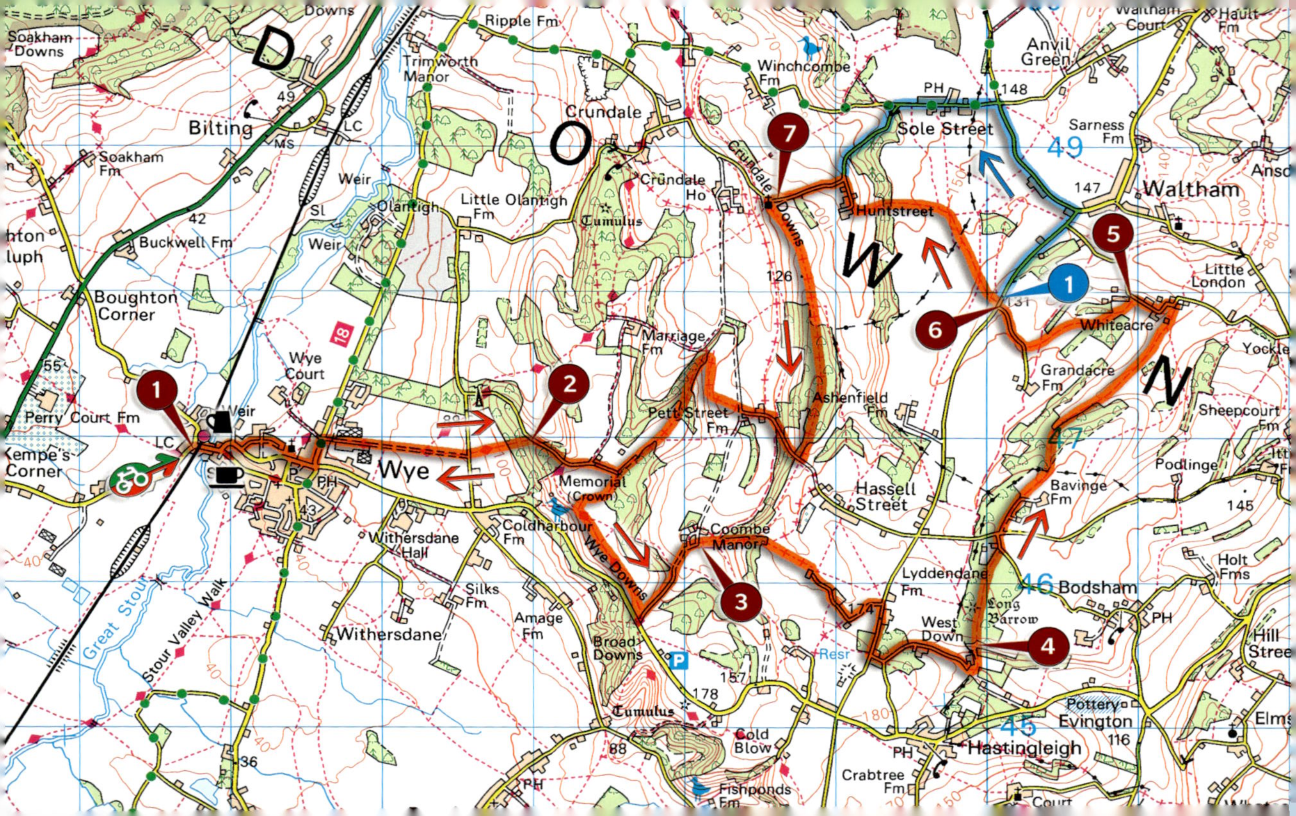
Soakham Downs
Ripple Fm
Trimworth Manor
Winchcombe Fm
Waltham Court
Hault Fm
Anvil Green
Crundale
Bilting
MS
LC
Soakham Fm
Weir
Olantigh
Little Olantigh Fm
Crundale Ho
Cumulus
Sole Street
PH
148
Sarness Fm
49
147
Waltham
Ansc
SL
42
Buckwell Fm
Huntstreet
Crundale Downs
Little London
Boughton Corner
Wye Court
126
131
Whiteacre
Yockle
Marriage Fm
Grandacre Fm
55
Perry Court Fm
Ashenfield Fm
Sheepcourt Fm
Kempe's Corner
Pett Street Fm
47
Wye
PH
43
Memorial (Crown)
Hassell Street
Podlinge
Bavinge Fm
145
Coldharbour Fm
Coombe Manor
Withersdane Hall
Lyddendane Fm
Holt Fms
Wye Downs
46
Bodsham
Great Stour
Stour Valley Walk
Silks Fm
Long Barrow
Amage Fm
Withersdane
174
West Down
PH
Hill Stree
Broad Downs
Resr
157
178
Pottery
Evington
Tumulus
45
116
Elms
Cold Blow
Hastingleigh
88
PH
Crabtree Fm
36
Fishponds Fm
Court
D
O
W
N

Directions

1 From **Wye station**, turn ← along Bridge Street and cross the bridge spanning the **Great Stour River**. Pass **The Tickled Trout** pub then turn ← at a fork and follow Churchfield Way around past **St Gregory and St Martin church** onto the High Street. Continue to another ✗ and turn ← onto Olantigh Road (*NCR 18 Canterbury*) and continue for 200m before turning → along Occupation Road (joining the NDW), a service road on the campus of Wye Agricultural College. Pass greenhouses, polytunnels and allotments and continue ↑ onto an arrow-straight bridleway track, climbing steadily. Cross a minor road and continue ↑ on a chalk/clay path, climbing more steeply across The Junipers before entering woods where the gradient becomes even steeper. Prominent tree roots give the climb an extra challenge.

2 Emerge from the woods and turn → onto a minor road and continue climbing. Where the gradient eases the NDW becomes a footpath and turns right off the road; continue ↑ along the road and at a fork by a house, bear → on a track road (green byway sign). Where the track road swings sharply left keep ↑ on the grassy track, go through a wooden gate into woods and turn sharply → here to join a bridleway (blue markers). Follow the bridleway along the edge of Collyer Hill Woods for 250m before turning ← through a metal bridlegate then immediately → to follow the fence around a field edge to a wooden bridlegate. Go through and turn ← to rejoin the NDW

Along the lovely grassy Wye Downs ridge

Glorious grassy valley by Bavinge Wood

bridleway where it runs along the edge of the Wye Downs ridge. After nearly 1km, go through a metal gate and shortly turn ← onto a minor road, leaving the NDW. Descend steeply along the narrow road and just before reaching **Coombe Manor**, turn → through a gate onto a bridleway.

3 Continue alongside a fence, turn ← through a bridlegate then shortly turn → to climb along a grassy byway track (red marker arrow). Go through a wooden gate at the edge of woodland, climb a little further then keep → at a fork. The track soon gives way to tarmac at Little Coombe, follow the lane through Smeed Farm and continue around to a T-junction. Turn → to continue past **Lyddendane Farm** then take the first **LH** turn after 400m (*Hastingleigh* and *Elmstead*). Take the first **LH** turn (no through road sign) and descend along a narrow lane; go through a gateway and continue ↑ to pass a large house. At a ✘ turn ← (bridleway signpost) and soon turn ← again to follow the bridleway (no signpost) between fences to the rear of the house. The path soon climbs very steeply – although fairly briefly – before levelling out and entering woods.

4 Continue along the woodland bridleway, which can be overgrown in summer and hoof-damaged after wet weather, keeping ↑ at a fork and eventually emerging at a minor road. Bear ← (↑) then at a T-junction, dogleg → then ← onto a farm track (green bridleway signpost) with a sign for **Bavinge Farm**. Where the track bends right towards the farm, keep ↑ on the bridleway track across a field (muddy after wet weather). At a fork bear ← (blue marker arrow – may be overgrown) and descend through Bavinge Wood. Go through a gate and continue along a beautiful grassy valley, eventually climbing a little to a metal bridlegate. Go through and follow the top edge of the field around to another metal gate, go through and turn ← along a narrow lane.

5 After 350m, turn ← (green bridleway sign) up a track towards a house. Bear ← by the garden gate to continue through woods (watch out for slippery roots). Where the bridleway emerges from the trees keep ↑ along a field edge before going through a metal bridlegate. Turn → along a hedgerow and continue to another metal bridlegate, go through and turn → along a narrow lane, soon descending to a T-junction.

6 Cross ↑ over the road and go around a metal barrier (blue marker arrow), climb along an arable field edge and where it bends sharply right, bear ← and head diagonally across the field (this can be tricky when crops are up). Once across continue ↑ (blue arrow marker) along a hedgerow and keep ↑ across another field when the hedgerow bends to the right. Once across, go through a gate into woodland and descend very steeply, passing through further gates and continuing down to a ✖ at **Huntstreet Farm**. Turn → and continue through the farm to arrive at a T-junction, turn ← and climb steadily.

Variant route after wet weather

1 If it has been rainy, parts of the route described in paragraph **6** can be seriously muddy. To avoid this, turn → and continue along the lane for 850m. Turn ← at a triangular junction, then ← again and continue for 1km to a ✖. Turn ← (*Sole Street* and *Crundale*) and continue through **Sole Street**. A little way beyond the village, turn ← by a large tree and descend steeply along a narrow lane. As the descent bottoms out, bear → and climb steadily for 500m.

7 At the brow of the hill pass by the flint-built **St Mary's Church** and turn ← onto a byway track (green byway sign). Continue along this excellent track with great views across **Crundale Downs**, climbing a little and passing around a metal gate before descending steadily; where the track emerges from the trees at the bottom of the descent, turn sharply → downhill on a

Zipping along the ridge, Crundale Downs

broad track. The descent bottoms out through **Pett Street Farm**. Continue ↑ climbing out of the farmyard on a concrete farm road. At a T-junction, dogleg → then ← onto a byway track. Follow the track around, enter woods, climb a little and continue to a byway ✗. Turn ← and climb steeply at length before the track levels and emerges from the woods. Pass Downs Farm and at a path ✗ turn → through a wooden gate. Continue along the track to rejoin the road and retrace your outward route to return to **Wye station**.

Descending through King's Wood (Route 16)

Byway track, Larkey Valley Wood

15

Route 15
Chartham Downs loop

START/FINISH	Larkey Valley car park TR 124 557; or Chartham train station TR 107 552
DISTANCE	20km (12½ miles)
ON ROAD	8.25km (5¼ miles)
OFF ROAD	11.75km (7¼ miles)
ASCENT	305m (1000ft)
GRADE	■
TIME	2hrs 30mins–3hrs
MAPS	OS Explorer 137 and 150, Landranger 179 and 189
PUB	The Compasses Inn at Sole Street
CAFÉ	None on the route, although Shelly's Tea Rooms in nearby Chilham is worth the detour

60%
OFF ROAD

Overview

This route links together some of the best byway and bridleway trails in the Chartham Downs area and for the most part uses narrow country lanes to link them together. Although relatively short and undemanding, the woodland bridleway paths can be very muddy and are fearsomely rutted in places; you will also need to pay attention to route-finding through Denge Wood in particular. If you have time to spare, there are way-marked singletrack trails to be enjoyed in Larkey Valley Wood by the start/finish point.

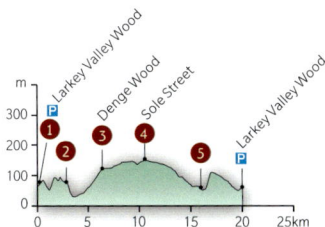

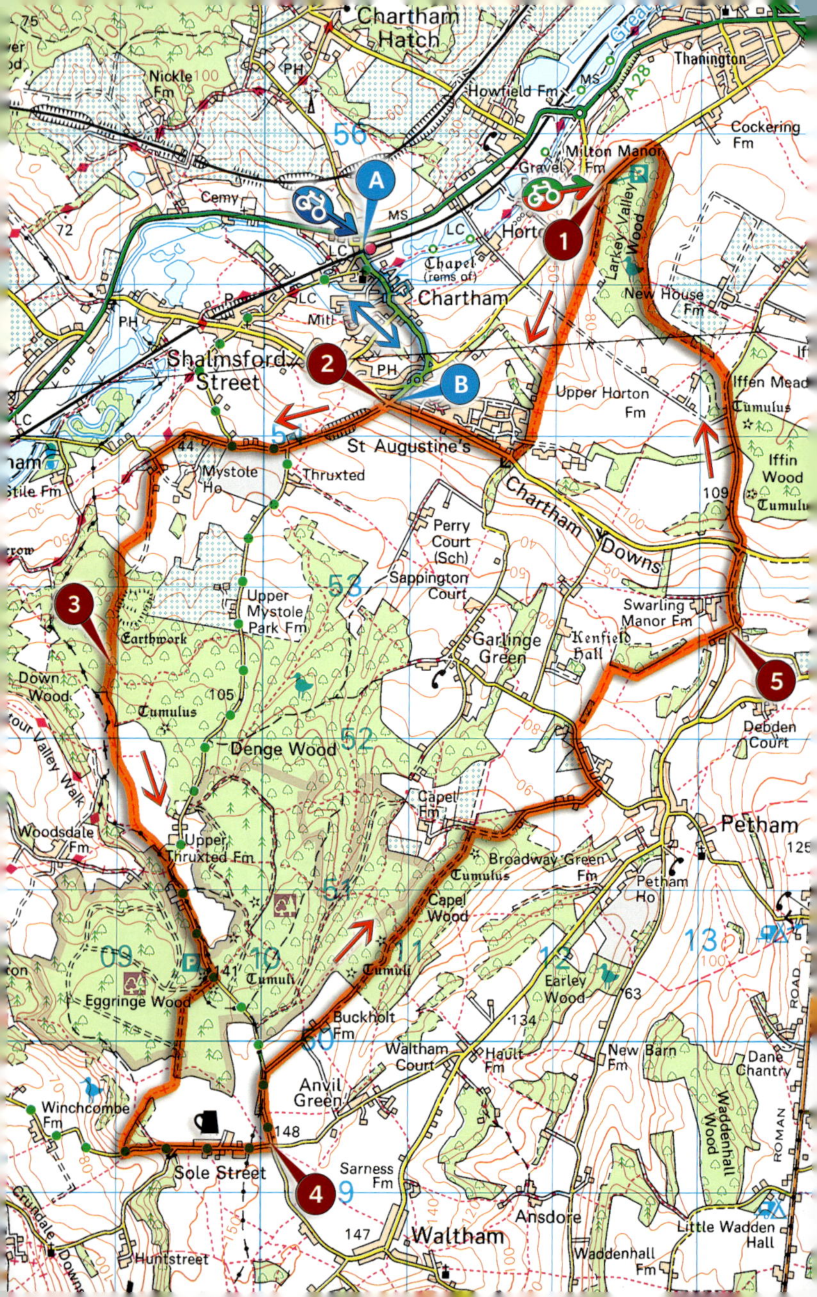

Chartham Hatch
Thanington
Nickle Fm
Howfield Fm
Cockering Fm
Milton Manor Fm
Gravel
Cemy
Horton
Chapel (rems of)
Chartham
Larkey Valley Wood
New House Fm
Mill
Shalmsford Street
Upper Horton Fm
Iffen Mead
Cumulus
Iffin Wood
St Augustine's
Mystole Ho
Thruxted
Chartham Downs
Stile Fm
Perry Court (Sch)
Sappington Court
Upper Mystole Park Fm
Swarling Manor Fm
Earthwork
Garlinge Green
Kenfield Hall
Down Wood
Cumulus
Debden Court
Stour Valley Walk
Denge Wood
Capel Fm
Petham
Woodsdale Fm
Upper Thruxted Fm
Broadway Green Fm
Petham Ho
Capel Wood
Cumuli
Eggringe Wood
Earley Wood
Buckholt Fm
Waltham Court
Hault Fm
New Barn Fm
Dane Chantry
Anvil Green
Winchcombe Fm
Waddenhall Wood
Sole Street
Sarness Fm
Ansdore
Waltham
Little Wadden Hall
Waddenhall Fm
Crundale Downs
Huntstreet
ROMAN ROAD
A 28
A
B
1
2
3
4
5

Directions

1 Follow the byway track running **S** from the **car park**, bearing **→** after 500m onto a narrow path where the main track runs into a large agricultural dump. The path descends alongside a fence then climbs through a narrow tunnel of hedges before emerging alongside a housing estate. Continue, crossing **↑** over a minor road to rejoin the byway (green byway sign), soon emerging onto another road. Turn **→** and continue for 1km to a **✕** before turning **←** onto Mystole Lane.

Alternative start from Chartham station

A Turn **←** onto Station Road (which becomes Rattington Street) and continue **↑** through the village. The road soon climbs out of the village. At a junction, turn **→** onto Cockering Road. At a mini roundabout, keep **↑** along Cockering Road. At a T-junction, continue **↑** onto Mystole Lane. This version adds 2.75km and 80m of ascent to the route.

2 Descend steeply along the lane and when the descent bottoms out continue **↑** at a fork (*Chilham*) along Mystole Road to a road/bridleway **✕**. Turn **←** onto a bridleway track road (green bridleway signpost), soon turning **→** past Barnyard Stables then continuing on a broad earth track past an agricultural shed and across a field, bearing **→** where the track forks. The bridleway soon enters woodland, keep **←** on the main track and after 1km watch out for a wooden post on your right with a blue bridleway way-marker; where the main track swings right, keep **↑** on a narrow path and go through a bridlegate (**TR 089 523**).

3 Continue **↑** for 300m, until the path forks. Keep **↑** (the left-hand path follows the edge of

Looking west across the Kent Downs near Denge Wood

Riding through arable fields near Denge Wood

Denge Wood) and make for a post in the middle of the field ahead. Continue ↑ on the bridleway (confusingly, there are only footpath way-markers on the post), go through a bridlegate, cross another field and go through another gate into woodland. Arriving at a road, turn →. After 800m turn → again onto a byway track opposite a parking area. Where the track forks, keep ← (there is a metal barrier to the right). Continue initially through woodland, then along a field edge. Where the path re-enters woodland take the **RH** path at a fork and descend to a road. Turn ← to climb along the road and pass the **Compasses Inn** at **Sole Street**.

④ At a ✗ turn ← on Penny Pot Lane (*Chartham*) and after 500m turn → onto a broad metalled track that makes for easy riding. After 2km, arrive at a T-junction with a narrow lane (Capel Road); turn → and arrive at another T-junction (opposite Wootton Barn) after 1km. Turn ← then after 500m turn → onto a bridleway along a field edge. Where the path reaches a gate, continue along a fence and descend to a road (Watery Lane).

⑤ Turn ← to climb and continue ↑ over a ✗ onto New House Lane. Continue along the road and 200m after passing the entrance to **Horton Farm** on the left, turn ← on a signposted bridleway that initially follows a field edge before entering **Larkey Valley Wood**. After 300m, turn → downhill at a fork (waymarker post) and continue ↑ for 800m to arrive at a small parking area on Cockering Road with a Larkey Valley Wood information panel. If you still have time and energy there are some good singletrack paths around Larkey Valley Wood (with colour-coded marker posts) to be enjoyed. To return to the **car park**, turn ← and continue uphill for 450m.

Alternative finish at Chartham station

B Follow the directions in paragraph **1**, then turn → onto Cockering Road. At the mini roundabout, go ↑ continuing on Cockering Road. Turn ← onto Rattington Street, which then becomes Station Road and turn → for the **station**.

Off-road trails through Larkey Valley Wood

Waterlogged bridleway, King's Wood

16

Route 16
Chilham and King's Wood loop

Start/Finish	Car park in Chilham TR 067 536; or Chilham train station TR 078 537
Distance	22km (13¾ miles)
On road	9km (5¾ miles)
Off road	13km (8 miles)
Ascent	350m (1150ft)
Grade	■
Time	2hrs 30mins–3hrs
Maps	OS Explorer 137, Landranger 179 and 189
Pub	The White Horse at Chilham
Café	Shelly's Tea Rooms at Chilham

60% OFF ROAD

Overview

Starting and finishing in the 'chocolate box' village of Chilham with its eponymous castle, this short, sweet route takes in a series of byways, bridleways (including a fine section of the NDW), forestry tracks and narrow lanes in a loop around King's Wood. Although bookended with considerable climbs and two excellent downhills near the end, this is a fairly level route – a very pleasant cruise through some lovely countryside. If you have the time, hours of fun can be had exploring the forestry tracks and singletrack trails snaking around King's Wood.

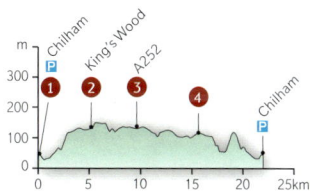

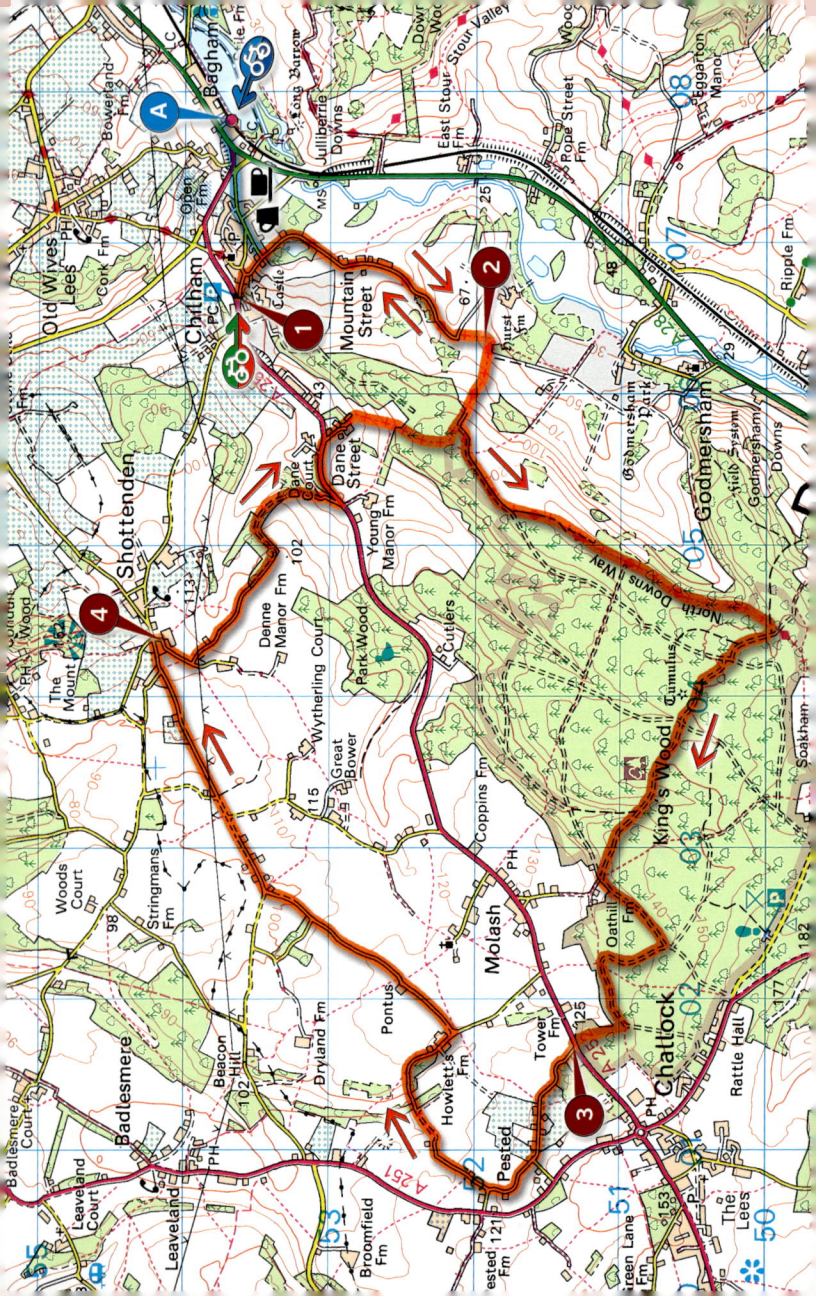

Directions

1 Exit **Chilham car park**, turn → and climb a little to the main square by **Chilham Castle**. Turn → (joining the NDW) to descend along School Hill then bear → at a T-junction onto Mountain Street.

Alternative start/finish at Chilham station

A Turn ← along the cycle path on the `A28` Canterbury Road. Continue ↑ over the next junction to follow the cycle path along the `A252`. Take the next **LH** turn and at the T-junction turn → along Bagham Lane. At a fork by **The Woolpack Inn**, turn ← along Hambrook Lane. At a T-junction/bend bear ← onto Mountain Street.

Follow the road around for 2km and where the tarmac gives way to a track that swings sharp left, keep ↑ past a metal gate by a small parking area to stay on the NDW along a tree-lined byway track.

2 Following the NDW, swing sharp → and climb fairly steeply; at the top of the climb bear ← at a fork to stay on the NDW. Continue ↑ along the broad, almost level woodland path for 3km then turn sharp → off the NDW onto a broad track (initially bearing **N**, then **NW**) through **King's Wood**. Keep ↑ over two ✗s before descending to a third ✗, climbing ↑ again then descending to a major track junction. Turn ← along the main track and continue for 600m to a ✗, turn → and continue along the track, which soon swings sharply **left**; after 400m turn → (N)

On the North Downs Way by King's Wood

At the top of the climb through Ridge Wood

along a track (not the footpath next to it) and follow this through the woods to arrive by the `A252`.

3 Cross ↑ over the road (with care) to continue along Pested Lane. At a T-junction by a triangle of grass, turn → and continue along a narrow farm road to Hegdale Farm. Continue past the farmhouse on a byway track; the byway crosses fields before entering a frequently overgrown sunken lane (this can be **easy to miss**). Climb a short way then continue ↑ through **Howlett's Farm**. Arriving at a road, turn ← (*Shottenden*) and continue to a T-junction. Turn → onto Shottenden Road and as you enter **Shottenden** at a ✖ turn → onto Denne Manor Lane.

4 After 300m, turn ← onto a byway track, initially on tarmac then along a deeply rutted grass track, which climbs steadily before descending steeply to arrive at a road. Turn ← along the `A252` (with care) for 400m before turning → onto a byway at **Dane Street**. The track soon climbs steeply through Ridge Wood. At the top of the climb, keep ↑ (←) at a fork. Continue to a T-junction with the NDW, turn ← and descend steeply, bearing sharp ← at the bottom, soon rejoining Mountain Street. For the alternative finish at Chilham station, turn → at Hambrook Lane and retrace the outward route. Otherwise, keep ↑ to return to **Chilham car park**.

Riding through Chilham village

Wintry weather in Tong Wood

17

Route 17

Rough Common–Blean Wood loop

START/FINISH	Canterbury West train station **TR 145 584**; or car park at Rough Common **TR 122 594**
DISTANCE	31.5km (19½ miles); or 29.75km (18½ miles)
ON ROAD	12.5km (7¾ miles); or 11.25km (7 miles)
OFF ROAD	19km (11¾ miles); or 18.5km (11½ miles)
ASCENT	440m (1445ft); or 410m (1345ft)
GRADE	■
TIME	3hrs–3hrs 30mins
MAPS	OS Explorer 149, Landranger 179 and 189
PUB	The Dove, Dargate
CAFÉ	Several in Canterbury

60%
OFF ROAD

Overview

The woodlands to Canterbury's northwest, a very short distance from the heart of the city, are one of the largest wooded areas in Kent. This route takes

full advantage of this and also heads south across the A2 to take in a collection of byways, bridleways and country lanes around Chartham Hatch before heading back into the city along the NDW. The ride includes a few ascents and descents with the climb up Holly Hill through Blean Wood being the most significant. Many of the forest trails can get fairly muddy during wet weather.

Much of the woodland to Canterbury's northwest is a (RSPB) National Nature Reserve, hence there are restrictions on cycling in some parts of Rough Common

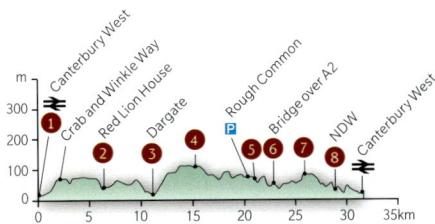

and Blean Woods. However, this route takes in some of the best accessible mountain biking trails in this area. There are plenty of other options to explore around these woods, including abundant singletrack trails – although navigation is an issue as most are unmarked. Please respect the 'no cycling' signs on some of the trails. The woods are popular with other users, so remember to slow down and give way as appropriate.

Directions

1 From **Canterbury West station**, turn ➜ onto the `A290` and head **NW** towards the outskirts of town, turning ➜ after 2km onto the Crab & Winkle Way (CWW) – *NCN1*.

Alternative start from Rough Common Nature Reserve car park

A Turn ⬅ and follow the access road back to the entrance, turn ⬅ and after 500m turn ➜ along the `A290`, jinking ⬅ onto the CWW – *NCN1* – after 150m.

Continue along the path, crossing a minor road and keeping ⬅ on the main path when a byway forks off to the right. Pass through Arbele Farm, with poly-tunnels on

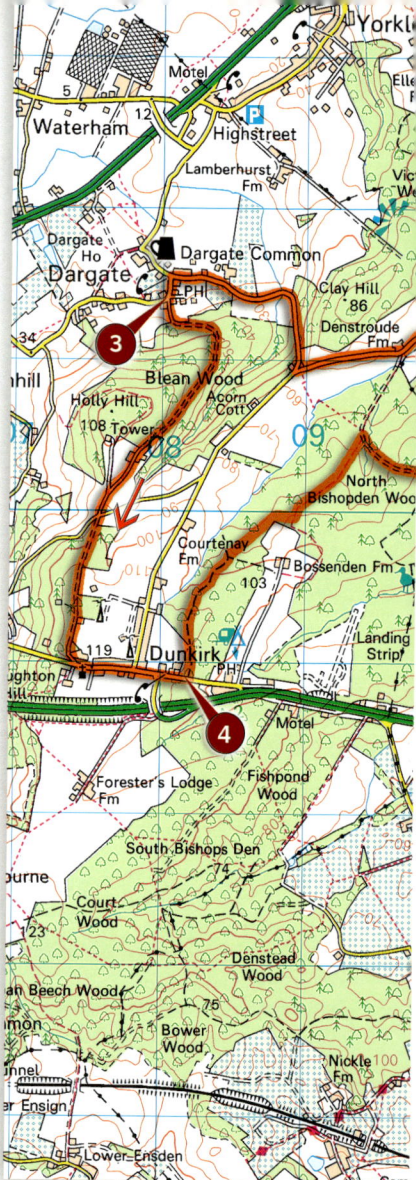

the left; keep ↑ (→ at a fork in the farmyard). Cross ↑ over a farm road continuing along the main bridleway, soon entering woodland. At a T-junction with a forestry road turn ← (leaving the CWW, which turns right). After 400m, descend on a gravel track through the woods. Where the descent bottoms out and the track swings left, jink → by an old stile (yellow marker), dismount and continue on the footpath soon crossing a grassy field.

Passing a Millennium Milepost on the Crab & Winkle Way

2 On reaching the **A290** by **Red Lion House**, turn → and after 400m turn ← (just past a nursery) onto Fox's Cross Road then immediately ← again onto a bridleway leading into woodland. At a fork, keep to the **LH** bridleway, climbing (hoof damage) through Tong Wood then descending gradually until you reach a minor road – Denstroude Lane; bear → along the road, which soon turns sharply **left**, and follow it past **Denstroude Farm** to a fork junction. Turn → (*Dargate* and *Hernhill*) and make the short, steep descent into **Dargate**, turning ← (*Hernhill* and *Boughton*) opposite **The Dove** pub.

3 After 150m, bear ← onto a bridleway (small horse symbol) by a white weather-boarded cottage. Climb steadily at length through **Blean Wood** on the Red Road track and continue through Holly Hill Farm to arrive at a minor road. Cross ↑ over the road onto another bridleway and continue through woods. Go through a gate before reaching the road at **Dunkirk**. Turn ← along the road for 600m, before keeping ← (*Canterbury* and *Dover A2*) at a bend. Shortly after passing a used car dealer, turn ← by a broken wooden gate to follow an unmarked path into woodland.

4 Continue ↑ – keeping ← at a fork – then descend a little to a T-junction. Turn → and follow the track around to a wooden barrier. Go through it then turn ← along a bridleway descending through woodland to arrive at a ✖ after 1.5km. Turn → (yellow marker) along the gravelled forest road and keep ↑ over all ✖s for 3.2km.

Shorter route variants

If you parked at Rough Common car park, you can shorten the route by turning ← off the gravelled forest road after 2.5km to return to it. If you wish to return to **Canterbury West station** from here, continue ↑ to arrive at a minor road. Turn ← and then bear → at the ✖ to join the A290, and follow the road for 2km. Taking either of these shorter routes would knock approximately 45mins–1hr off the ride time.

5 Turn → onto the path into woodland, opposite the rugby pitch. Descend then turn → onto a bridleway at a T-junction. Descend, cross a small stream then climb again; at the fork take the **LH** track. Bear → (↑) at the next path intersection and follow the singletrack path until you reach a post on the **RH** side of the path, which is **easily missed**. Turn ← at the post, and continue downhill on a fast, often muddy track to arrive at a minor road. Turn ← then almost immediately → by a white weather-boarded house onto a tree-lined bridleway. Cross a bridge with a decrepit gate to emerge into a small field. Bear → across the field and continue through a gate and stay on the path all of the way up to the T-junction with a road.

6 Turn ← and cross the road bridge over the A2. Turn ← again and continue down a farm road. Where a bridleway forks left, stay with the road, then bear round to the → and continue past a couple of large houses at **Poldhurst Farm**. The road becomes a track as it passes several large barns; keep ↑ along the track through the orchards passing through a couple of gateways. The track passes **Denstead Farm** before emerging on Denstead Lane. Turn ← along the road for 400m before turning → through a gateway (green byway sign) that leads into an orchard. Bear ← to follow the byway along the orchard's edge. Pass by a footpath on the left then just before a right-hand bend, bear ← on a

Riding through orchards near Chartham Hatch

track leading through trees out onto a minor road. Turn ← and climb steeply along Primrose Hill. At the top of the climb turn ← at a junction (*Harbledown* and *Dunkirk*) and continue to a ✖ in **Chartham Hatch**.

7 Continue ↑ onto Bigbury Road. After 700m turn → onto a bridleway track road (green *KCC* sign with walker symbol) and continue, initially through houses. By a 'private property' sign take the narrow track that leads to the **left** of the fence; this soon opens out as the bridleway climbs then descends a little to arrive at the corner of a minor road. Bear ← (↑) and continue along Tonford Lane keeping ↑ (→) past a left-hand turning after 400m. At a fork bear → downhill onto Faulkner's Lane, soon crossing the **A2** on a road bridge.

Alternative finish at Rough Common car park

B Continue along Faulkner's Lane for 500m before turning ← to reach a T-junction with the **A2050**. Turn → and continue along the eastbound carriageway for 200m before turning ← (*Rough Common* and *Blean*) onto Palmars Cross Hill. Climb steeply then continue for 1.2km into **Rough Common**; turn ← by a bus stop (RSPB sign – *Blean Wood Nature Reserve*) and take the minor road on the **RH** side to return to the **car park**.

8 Turn → and go around a gate to join and follow the **NDW** bridleway track, which runs parallel to the **A2** for 500m before it veers **left** on a sunken lane between fields. Cross a footbridge. At a ✖ keep ↑ on the bridleway, following *NDW* signs and passing behind houses. The NDW eventually joins a residential street (Mill Lane) before emerging next to a roundabout. Go around the roundabout and take the exit by the Victoria Hotel. Continue along London Road to a T-junction with a mini-roundabout; turn → then, after 300m, turn ← to arrive at **Canterbury West station**.

Nearing the top of the steep climb up Tolsford Hill (Route 18)

Routes around Elham and Temple Ewell

Near the top of the climb, Covert Wood

Route 18
Elham Valley loop

START/FINISH	Elham **TR 177 439**; or Sandling train station **TR 148 368**
DISTANCE	23km (14 miles); or 41.75km (26 miles)
ON ROAD	11.5km (7 miles); or 23.25km (14½ miles)
OFF ROAD	11.5km (7 miles); or 18.5km (11½ miles)
ASCENT	445m (1460ft); or 830m (2725ft)
GRADE	▲ ◆ (if following alternative start/finish)
TIME	3hrs–3hrs 30mins; or 5hrs 30mins–6hrs 30mins
MAPS	OS Explorer 138, Landranger 179 and 189
PUB	The Rose and Crown and The King's Arms, Elham
CAFÉ	The Cosy Tea Rooms of Elham

Overview

The Elham Valley is a hidden gem tucked away in the East Kent countryside. The main route described here loops around the ridges enclosing the valley to west and east, taking in bridleways, byways and narrow country lanes weaving through atmospheric woodlands. Although a significant proportion of the route is on tarmac, most of the roads involved can be described as very 'rustic' and see little traffic. The countryside in these parts is sublime; Elham itself has been Kent Village of the Year in recent times and it's easy to see why – half-timbered houses, a fine church and several excellent pubs congregate in a truly idyllic setting.

The main route is not especially challenging, although there's a fair amount of climbing involved; when combined with the variant route, however, this is quite a tough undertaking. The climb up Tolsford Hill is a leg-sapping lung-buster and descending the same hill on the return leg makes for a fairly nerve-wracking experience.

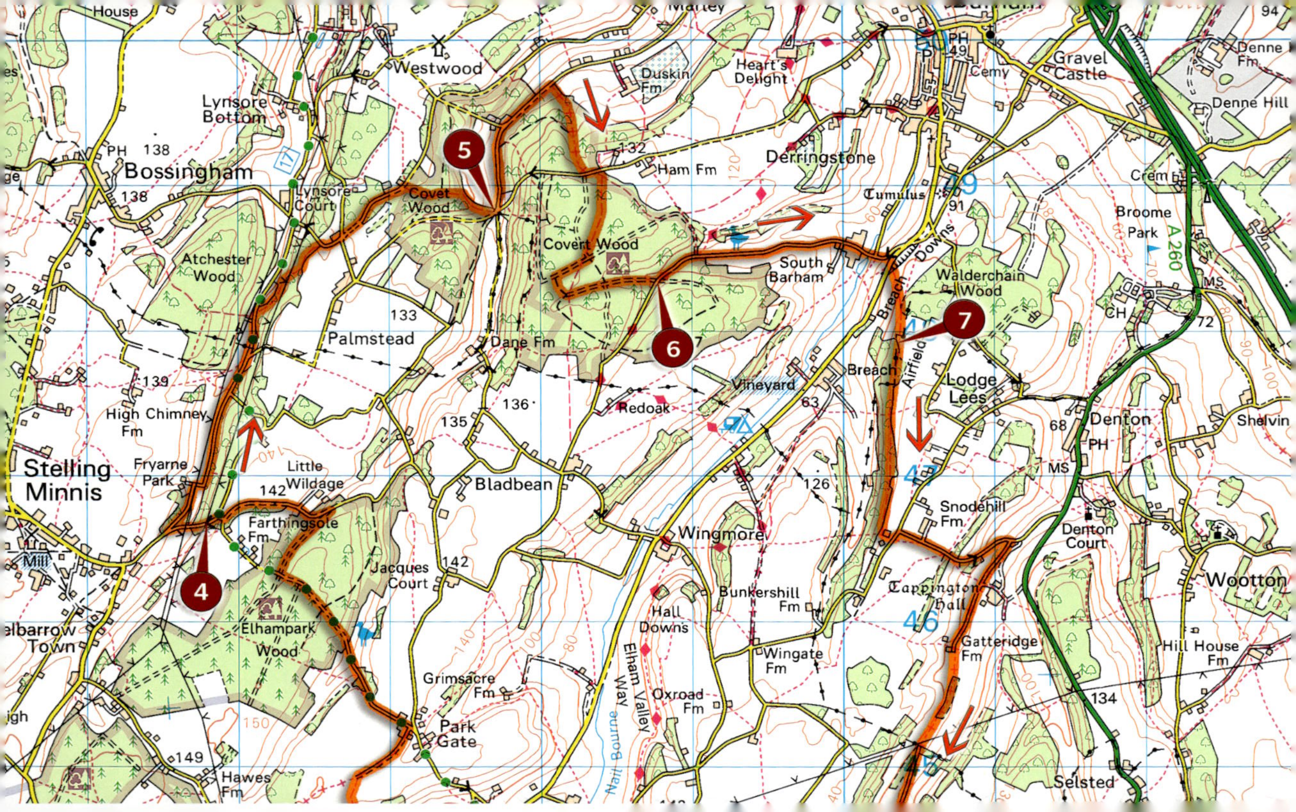

Westwood
Lynsore Bottom
Bossingham
Lynsore Court
Covet Wood
Covert Wood
Atchester Wood
Palmstead
Dane Fm
Duskin Fm
Heart's Delight
Derringstone
Ham Fm
Gravel Castle
Denne Fm
Denne Hill
Cemy
Crem
Broome Park
A 260
Tumulus
South Barham
Walderchain Wood
Breach Downs
Airfield
Lodge Lees
Breach
Vineyard
Redoak
High Chimney Fm
Stelling Minnis
Fryarne Park
Little Wildage
Bladbean
Farthingsole Fm
Jacques Court
Elhampark Wood
Wingmore
Bunkershill Fm
Hall Downs
Elham Valley Way
Nail Bourne
Oxroad Fm
Wingate Fm
Grimsacre Fm
Park Gate
Hawes Fm
Snodehill Fm
Denton
Denton Court
Shelvin
Wootton
Tappington Hall
Gatteridge Fm
Hill House Fm
Selsted
Mill
Town
1
2
3
4
5
6
7

Directions

Alternative start from Sandling station

A Cross the station car park to the **SE** corner and follow the footpath along the course of a dismantled railway line for 400m, then carry your bike up a long series of steps climbing above a disused **tunnel**. At the top, continue along the footpath a short way to a ✖ with a bridleway. Turn ← and follow the track around to a ✖ with a minor road, continue ↑ and cross a bridge over railway lines and then a second bridge over the M20. Continue ↑ to arrive at a ✖ with the A20. Turn ← along the road (with care) for 100m before turning → onto a byway track road.

B Follow the track road, which is fairly level at first, to the foot of **Tolsford Hill** where it becomes a flint and dirt track that climbs steadily to begin with, but soon becomes very steep with the added challenge of deep ruts and huge flints to negotiate. It is a tough old climb, but happily you will have to dismount half way up to go through a gate. The second stage of the climb is equally tough and you will be doing well to get to the top without pushing. The summit is marked with an OS trig point and the huge tower of **Swingfield Radio Station** looms beyond. Pedal past the tower to a gate, go through and descend ↑ along the **LH** option of two tracks. The track joins Westfield Lane and continues through **Etchinghill** to a ✖.

C Continue ↑ soon climbing steeply along Teddars Leas Road; soon after the climb levels take a **LH** fork (*Acrise* and *Shuttleswood*). The road soon descends then climbs steeply again; shortly after the top of the climb the road joins **National Cycle Route 17** (NCR17). Continue ↑ then keep → at a fork, arriving at a ✖ after 400m. Turn ← (*Elham*) and descend along the road to arrive at another ✖. Keep ⬆ and soon descend steeply along a narrow lane (**check your speed**), which bottoms out as it enters **Elham**. The road climbs gently again. Keep ⬆ over a ✖, turn ➡ at the following T-junction then bear ⬅ after 100m and climb briefly along Cullen's Lane. Now follow the route description in paragraph **②**.

● ●

① From the car park by the **church** with the **King's Arms** behind you, follow the lane to the **RH** side of the church and continue to a T-junction; turn ➡. Continue ⬆ over a ✖ and at the following T-junction, turn ➡. After 150m turn ⬅ and climb briefly along Cullen's Lane.

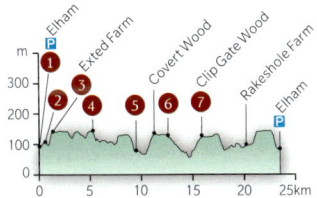

② Shortly after the road begins descending, turn ➡ onto an unsignposted right of way along a sunken lane. The path emerges briefly along a field edge before climbing very steeply along a flinty sunken lane. The path then emerges onto a minor road; turn ➡ and then ⬅ into Exted Farm (*Bridleway*).

③ Dogleg ⬅ then continue ⬆ through the farm buildings and go through a gate. The path swoops down then up across pasture land and arrives at a gate; go through and continue ⬆ to another gate. Go through and turn ➡ along a byway track for 500m to arrive at a minor road by Upper Park Gate Farm. Turn ⬅ and continue along a country lane, descending then climbing again as the road enters **Elhampark Wood**. As the road descends briefly again, turn ➡ onto a forestry track;

Surveying the English Channel from Tolsford Hill

Rolling pasture land near Exted Farm

continue ↑ for 600m to arrive at a minor road. Turn ← and climb along the lane for 750m to a ✖. Turn → (*NCN17*) then ← at the T-junction (*Stelling Minnis*).

④ Descend steeply then climb again; at a T-junction turn sharp → and continue along a lovely lane following the valley floor for almost 2km before turning → onto a bridleway (**signpost easy to miss**) and climbing gently across meadowland. The path enters woodland, becomes more defined and climbs steeply. At the top of the climb, turn → on a minor road, then at a ✖ at Clambercrown (*Bursted Manor* and *Bridge*) dogleg ← then immediately bear → at a fork (the left-hand option is unsuitable for motor vehicles); after 500m turn → onto a bridleway (Forestry Commission sign: *Covet Wood*) opposite Kingswood Farm. Climb a little through **Covet Wood** keeping ↑ at a ✖ before descending steeply on a broad track. At the bottom of the descent emerge onto a minor road at a ✖.

⑤ Take the **LH** road (Covet Lane – *Kingston*) and after 1km turn → into **Covert Wood** on a signposted byway. Climb fairly steeply along the flint-cobbled track, which can be slippery after rain. At the top of the climb, turn ← on a minor road for 100m, then turn → onto a bridleway – taking the **RH** fork. The path can be very wet and muddy after rain. Emerge onto a metalled forestry track, turn ← along the track, then → shortly after; bearing ← at the next fork. Stay with the main track where it swings right (ignoring the dirt track straight ahead), soon descending to a ✖ with a minor road (South Barham Hill) beyond a metal barrier.

6 At the ✖ turn ← and follow the lane as it descends through Covert Wood then continue along a picturesque valley to South Barham Farm before climbing steeply to a T-junction at **Breach Downs**. Cross the road and look out for a bridleway track (no signpost initially) on the right-hand side of a layby. Follow this to a field edge; a bridleway signpost on the road below points diagonally across the field. Follow the vague path steeply uphill across the field to a gate.

7 Go through and continue through Clip Gate Wood on an initially narrow path. After 1.5km, emerge onto a minor road. Turn ← then almost immediately →. Continue ↑ and soon descend steeply. At a ✖ at the bottom of the descent, turn → onto Rakeshole Lane, and continue along the valley floor for 2.5km on a good track, passing by **Rakeshole Farm**. Turn → along a minor road, soon climbing steeply. At the top of the climb, turn ← and continue for 650m to **Standardhill Farm**. To return to **Elham**, take the **RH** fork and soon descend steeply to arrive back at the village.

Alternative finish at Sandling station

· ·

D Take the **LH** fork at **Standardhill Farm**. After 2km, turn ← at a T-junction (*Shuttlesfield* and *Acrise*); continue ↑ over a ✖ and then turn → at a second ✖. Keep ↑ over a ✖ at **Shuttlesfield** and continue for 1.6km before bearing → (↑) onto Teddars Leas Road. Descend to a ✖ in Etchinghill and cross ↑ onto Westfield Lane. Climb along the lane, bearing → at a track fork after 350m. At the top of the climb cross over the road and go through a stockgate. Follow the access track past Swingfield Radio Station before forking ← (↑) onto the earth track. Go through a gate and descend the steep, rutted and flinty flank of **Tolsford Hill**. As the gradient eases keep ↑ on the byway track before reaching the A25. Turn ← along the road (with care) for 100m. Turn → and follow the SSW over bridges across the M20 and the **Eurostar railway line**. At a ✖ keep ↑ along the SSW for 500m before turning → onto a footpath. Dismount and follow the path a short way before descending steps and continuing along a dismantled railway line to return to **Sandling station**.

· ·

Route 19

Alkham–Barham Downs loop

19

START/FINISH	Kearsney train station **TR 289 440**; Kearsney Abbey car park **TR 289 438**
DISTANCE	40.5km (25 miles)
ON ROAD	17.75km (11 miles)
OFF ROAD	22.75km (14 miles)
ASCENT	745m (2445ft)
GRADE	▲
TIME	3hrs–4hrs
MAPS	OS Explorer 138, Landranger 179 and 189
PUB	The Black Robin, Kingston; The Two Sawyers, Woolage Green
CAFÉ	Kearsney Abbey Tea Rooms

55% OFF ROAD

Overview

This fine circular route ranges far and wide across the east Kent downs, starting and finishing at Temple Ewell in the southeast

with Barham Downs at its northeastern limit. The route shares some of its DNA with Routes 18 and 20, but is combined with a plethora of other byways, bridleways and lanes to create an entirely distinctive ride through some lovely rolling countryside.

This is quite a tough ride with a number of challenging climbs; most of these are in the first half of the route with the two toughest climbs coming early on. By contrast, the latter part of the ride is more of a relaxed affair following the NDW for much of the way before descending back to Temple Ewell at the end.

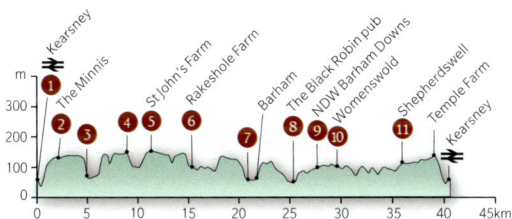

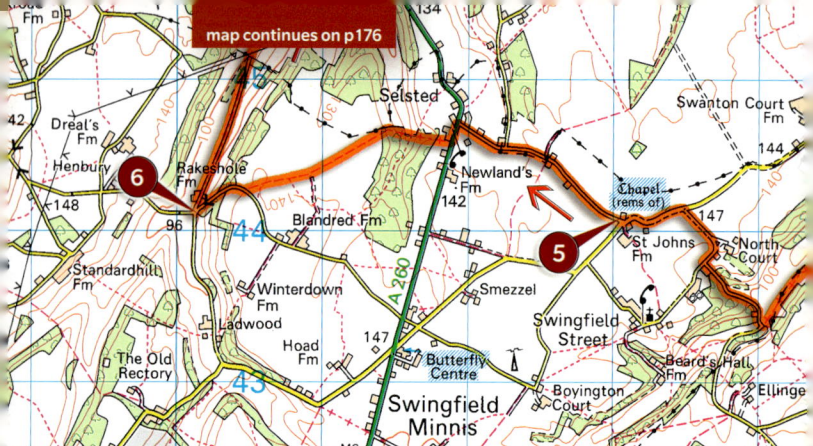

map continues on p176

Directions

1 Exit **Kearsney station** car park and turn ➔ onto the Alkham Road. Go under a railway bridge, keep ➔ at a fork then just past a **RH** turn (*Temple Ewell*), turn ➔ by a flint-built house (green byway signpost).

Alternative start at Kearsney Abbey car park

A Turn ➔ along the Alkham Road then take the **LH** turn by an imposing flint-built house (green byway signpost).

Pass a street sign (*Scotland Common*), then climb steeply and at length along the narrow tarmac lane; where the climb levels, tarmac gives way to a rutted (often muddy) earth track. Continue through woods then go through a stock gate to follow the track along the edge of woods fringing **The Minnis common**.

2 At the far (W) end of the common, continue ↑ through a gate onto a restricted byway track. After 600m turn ← by some houses and continue along a lane for 500m before arriving at a ✖. Bear ← past a red telephone box and dogleg ← and then ➔ onto Green Lane – a restricted byway with a green bridleway sign. Continue along the track road, which eventually passes a house (watch out for goats and geese!), turns sharp ← and becomes very narrow as it runs alongside a fence – this path can be very overgrown in summer. Pass through a gate and descend across an open

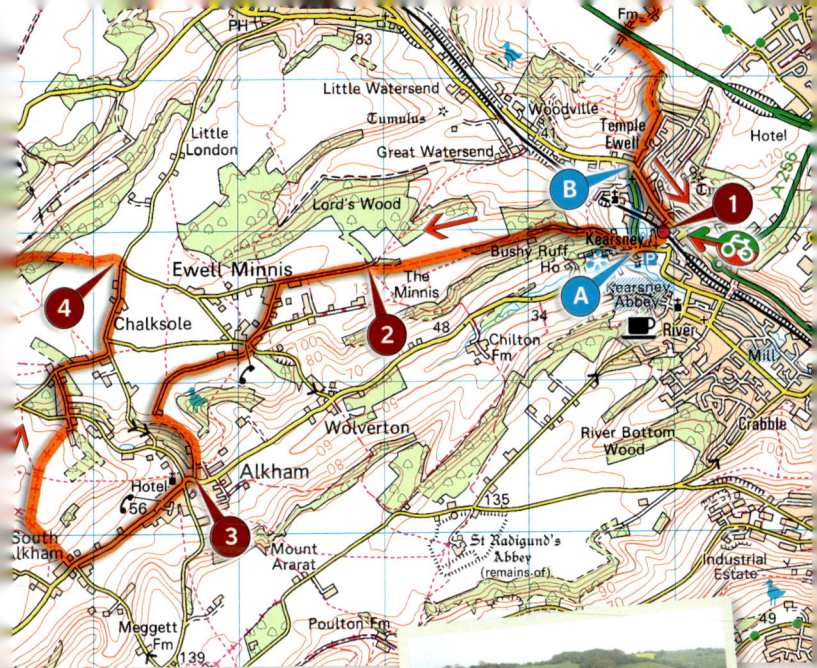

hillside with fine views over Alkham. Make for a gate, go through and continue descending.

3 Arriving at Alkham Valley Road, turn → and continue through **Alkham**, keeping ↑ at a ✖ then turning → onto a byway track after 1km. The flinty track soon climbs very steeply; keep → at a fork near the top of the climb. Go through a gate and continue along a field edge on a rutted path that can be very muddy. Descend steeply

Rolling country at Alkham on the Kent Downs

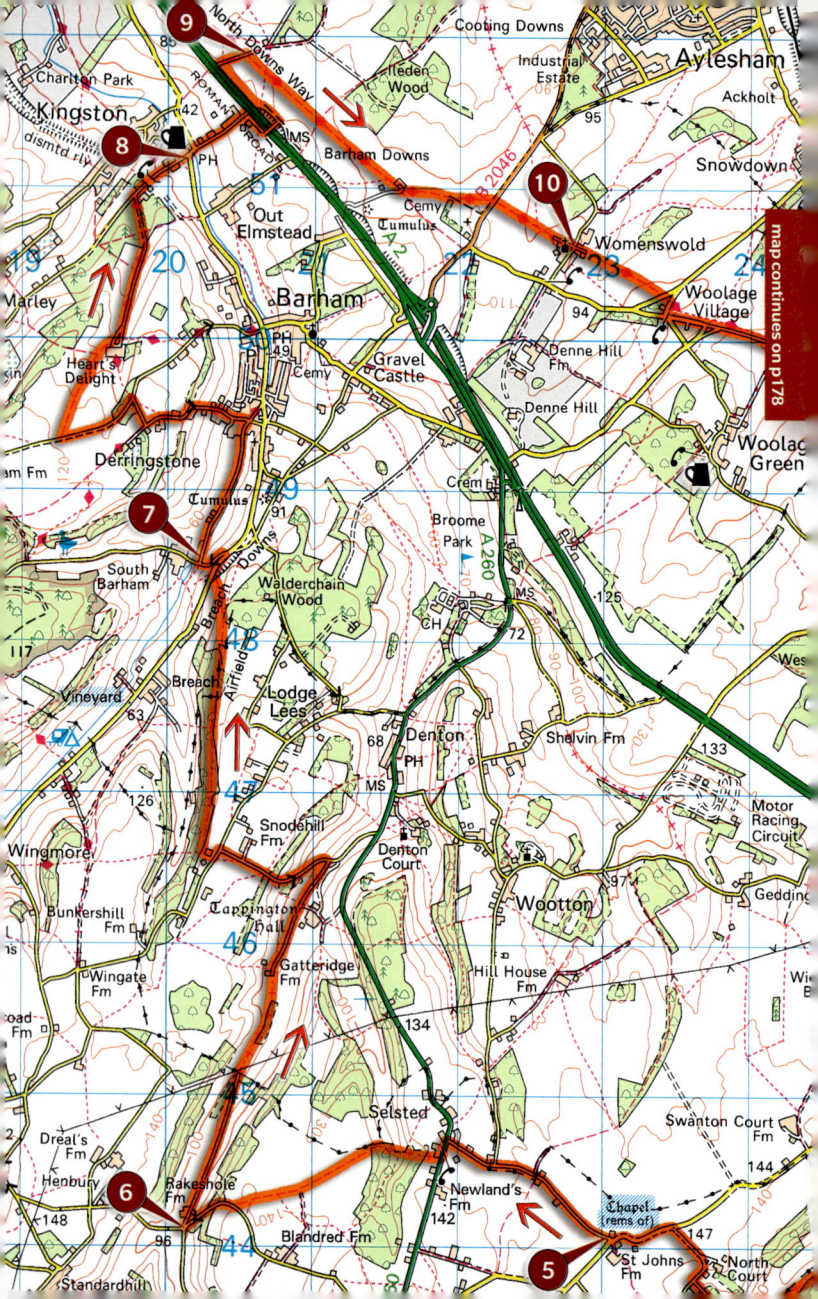

map continues on p178

Loose flints on the descent to Slip Lane

to cross a minor road (Slip Lane – green byway signpost) and immediately start climbing again on a steep-sided flinty track with the added challenge of a very deep rut along the middle. You'll be doing well to reach the top without getting (or falling) off and pushing! At the top turn ➔ along a minor road and continue to a T-junction. Turn ← along Warren Lane, continue ↑ past one right-hand turn, then turn ← onto a byway track just past a second right-hand turn.

4 Cross open fields to a gate, go through and soon descend steeply on a sunken lane through Fidge's Wood. At the bottom of the descent, go through a stock gate and cross to the bottom edge of the field, bearing ← (**SW**) to continue on the byway. Go through a gate at the field edge and turn ➔ onto a minor road. Climb steeply to a T-junction, turn ➔ and follow the road around a sharp **LH** bend to another T-junction. Turn ←.

5 After 500m turn ➔ opposite **St Johns Farm** onto a narrow lane and continue along the lane for 1.4km. At a T-junction with the **A260**, turn ← to pass several houses then turn ➔ onto a track (green byway sign). Descend through woodland on a rough track strewn with loose flints, keep ↑ (➔) at a path ✖ then climb fairly steeply. Emerge from the woods, bear ➔ along a grassy field edge then turn ← to follow a bridleway cutting diagonally across an arable field; enter a small copse then turn ➔ through a gap to continue diagonally across another field. Arrive at a minor road, turn ➔ and descend steeply.

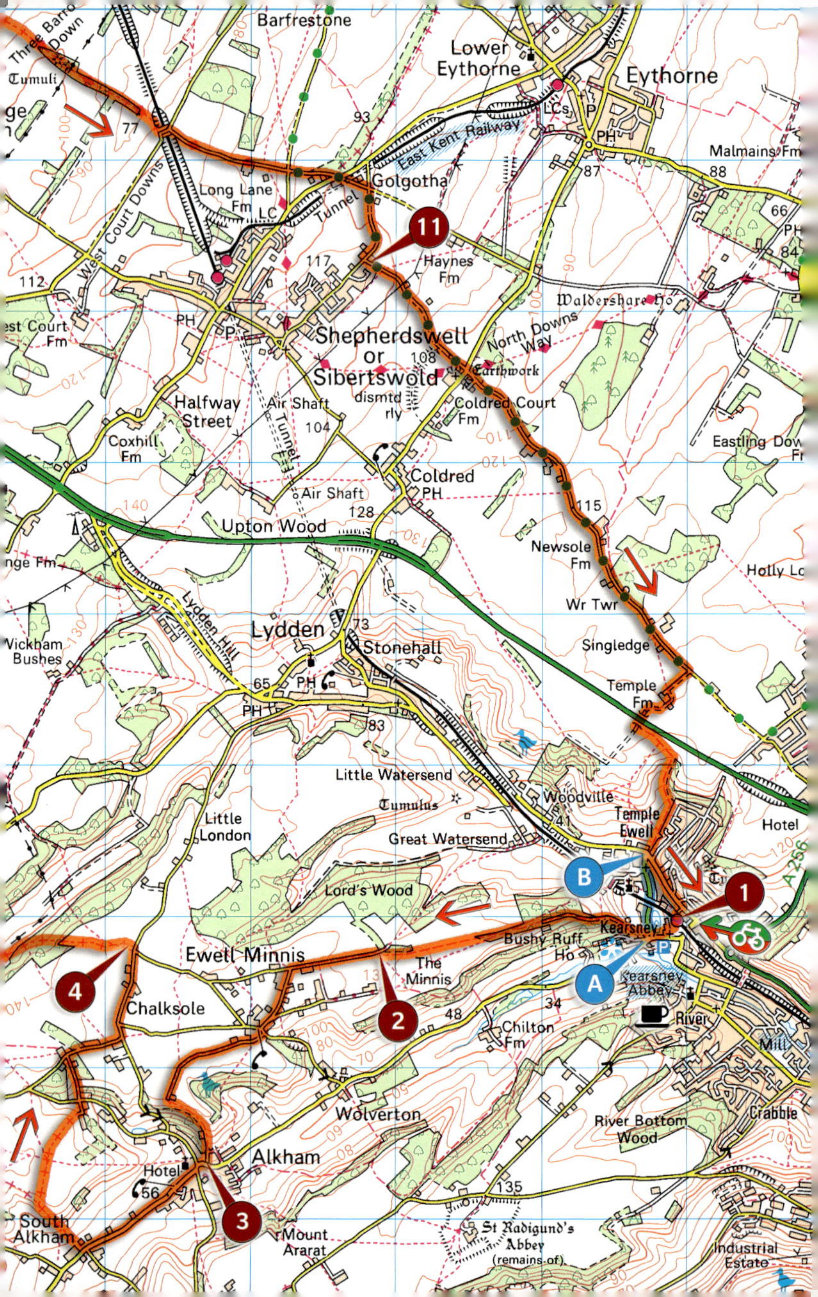

Three Barrow Down
Tumuli
Barfrestone
Lower Eythorne
Eythorne
77
93
Malmains Fm
East Kent Railway
Golgotha
87
88
Long Lane Fm
LC
Tunnel
11
117
Haynes Fm
66
PH
84
West Court Downs
112
Waldershare Ho
est Court Fm
PH
P
Shepherdswell or Sibertswold
108
North Downs Way
Earthwork
Halfway Street
120
Air Shaft
104
dismtd rly
Coldred Court Fm
110
Eastling Dow Fr
Coxhill Fm
140
Tunnel
Coldred PH
120
Upton Wood
128
Air Shaft
115
Newsole Fm
Holly Lo
130
Lydden Hill
Lydden
73
Stonehall
Wr Twr
Singledge
65
PH
PH
83
Temple Fm
Vickham Bushes
Little Watersend
Woodville
Tumulus
Temple Ewell
Hotel
Little London
Great Watersend
B
Hotel
Lord's Wood
1
A 256
4
Ewell Minnis
The Minnis
Bushy Ruff Ho
Kearsney
2
48
Kearsney Abbey
P
A
Chalksole
Chilton Fm
34
River
Wolverton
River Bottom Wood
Crabble
Hotel
56
Alkham
135
South Alkham
3
Mount Ararat
St Radigund's Abbey (remains of)
Industrial Estate
Mill

6 At the ✖ at the bottom of the descent, turn ➔ onto a farm road (green byway sign), passing **Rakeshole Farm** and continuing along the valley for 2.5km on a good track. At a T-junction with a minor road, turn ← onto Snode Lane and climb very steeply. After the gradient eases, continue to a T-junction, turn ← then almost immediately turn ➔ onto a bridleway path just past a house. The path soon bears **right** and continues along a wooded ridge for 1.5km, narrowing before exiting the woods through a gate. The bridleway descends diagonally across the flank of **Breach Downs** to arrive by a road. Follow the track alongside the road and into a layby before crossing the road and turning ← down the South Barham Hill road. Descend a short way then turn ➔ along South Barham Road.

7 Continue along the lane (prone to flooding) to a T-junction at **Barham**. Turn ← onto Railway Hill and climb steeply along the winding lane, which levels then turns sharply **right** before reaching a T-junction. Turn ← onto Greenhills and continue along the lane for 500m before turning ➔ onto a grassy track (green bridleway sign). Keep ↑ (➔) at a path ✖ then pass by the orchard and twin oast houses at **Heart's Delight Farm**. Bear ← then ← again to

Heading along the valley floor on Rakeshole Lane

Womenswold on the North Downs Way

join the Elham Valley Way (EVW). Continue along a farm road, which enters woods and descends steadily before arriving at a T-junction. Turn ➜ along a minor road, pass under an old railway bridge and continue to a junction with Valley Road.

8 Bear ⬅ (⬆), pass **The Black Robin** pub, turn ➜ (⬆) and climb steadily along Black Robin Lane. On emerging at the busy **A2**, turn ➜ to climb gently along a path running parallel to the road. Ignore a path descending on the left and continue to climb before turning ⬅ to cross over the **A2** on an impressive footbridge. Turn ⬅ and follow the tarmac bridleway for 650m before turning ➜ onto a farm road for 200m.

9 Turn ➜ to join the **NDW**. The path crosses an arable field (can be muddy) before joining a broad grassy track. Continue ⬆ for 1km or so and leave the track to continue ⬆ (blue bridleway waymarker) as you pass by Upper Digges Farm. Turn ⬅ at a path ✖, go round a metal stock gate then turn ➜ onto a track by a barn. Continue ⬆ then fork ⬅ off the main track (blue waymaker), cutting across a field to reach the `B2046`. Cross the road ↑ to continue along the NDW on a bridleway, keeping ← at a fork.

⑩ Soon arriving in the beautiful little hamlet of **Womenswold**, dogleg ← then → across the road to continue along a bridleway (*NDW*); pass a house, dogleg ← through a gap then → to continue along a field edge. On reaching a road cross ↑ through a copse (green *NDW* sign) onto another road. Turn → (briefly leaving the NDW, which becomes footpath) and continue to a ✖. Turn ← (*Barfrestone* and *Eythorne*) and continue ↑ past **Woolage Village**, bearing ← (↑) at a T-junction. Where the road bears sharply left, keep ↑ to join a tree-lined track (green *NDW* sign) and climb steadily. The track descends gently then climbs a little before turning → onto a broader track. Turn ← onto a minor road crossing a railway bridge, then immediately turn → along Long Lane (green *NDW* sign). After 700m the NDW turns right along a footpath; leave it here and keep ↑ over two ✖s (joining NCN16) and at a third ✖, turn → by a timber yard. Continue towards **Shepherdswell**, but take the first **LH** turn (*Coldred*).

⑪ Continue for 1km and then keep ↑ over a ✖ (*Whitfield* and *Dover*) then stay with the winding road for a further 2.5km before turning → along a farm road to **Temple Farm**. On approaching the farmhouse, bear ← to skirt the property and follow the track around to go through an underpass beneath the `A2`. Turn ← through a gate, continue diagonally across grazing pasture and go through another gateway. Bear → and descend to go through another gate at the top of a tree-lined bridleway path. Descend steeply – the path becomes narrow, awkward and overgrown in summer as it passes behind garden fences. Emerge at the road by the former George and Dragon pub. Turn ← along London Road and follow signs to **Kearsney station**.

Alternative finish at Kearsney Abbey car park

Ⓑ At the road by the former George and Dragon pub, cross ↑ onto High Street to continue to the car park at **Kearsney Abbey**.

Climbing the escarpment between Alkham and River

20

Route 20

Temple Ewell loop

Start/Finish	Kearsney train station **TR 289 440**; or Kearsney Abbey car park **TR 289 438**
Distance	34.75km (21¾ miles)
On road	14.75km (9¼ miles)
Off road	20km (12½ miles)
Ascent	585m (1920ft)
Grade	◆
Time	3hrs 30mins–4hrs
Maps	OS Explorer 138, Landranger 179 and 189
Pub	The Railway Bell, Kearsney
Café	Kearsney Abbey Tea Rooms

60%
OFF ROAD

Overview

This route makes the most of some of the best bridleway and byway tracks to the northwest of Dover. After a long climb out of Temple Ewell at the start, most of the tough climbs are reserved for the latter half of the route. Tricky ascents on steep flinty tracks are rewarded with some long, rattling descents. Although over a third of the route is on tarmac, the roads involved are mostly narrow country lanes through some very lovely rolling, wooded countryside – with the added bonus of very little traffic.

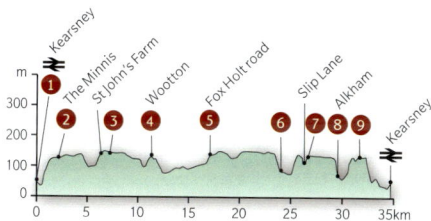

Directions

1. Exit **Kearsney station** car park and turn ➜ onto the Alkham Road. Go under a railway bridge, keep ➜ at a fork then just past a right-hand turn (*Temple Ewell*), turn ➜ by a flint-built house (green byway signpost).

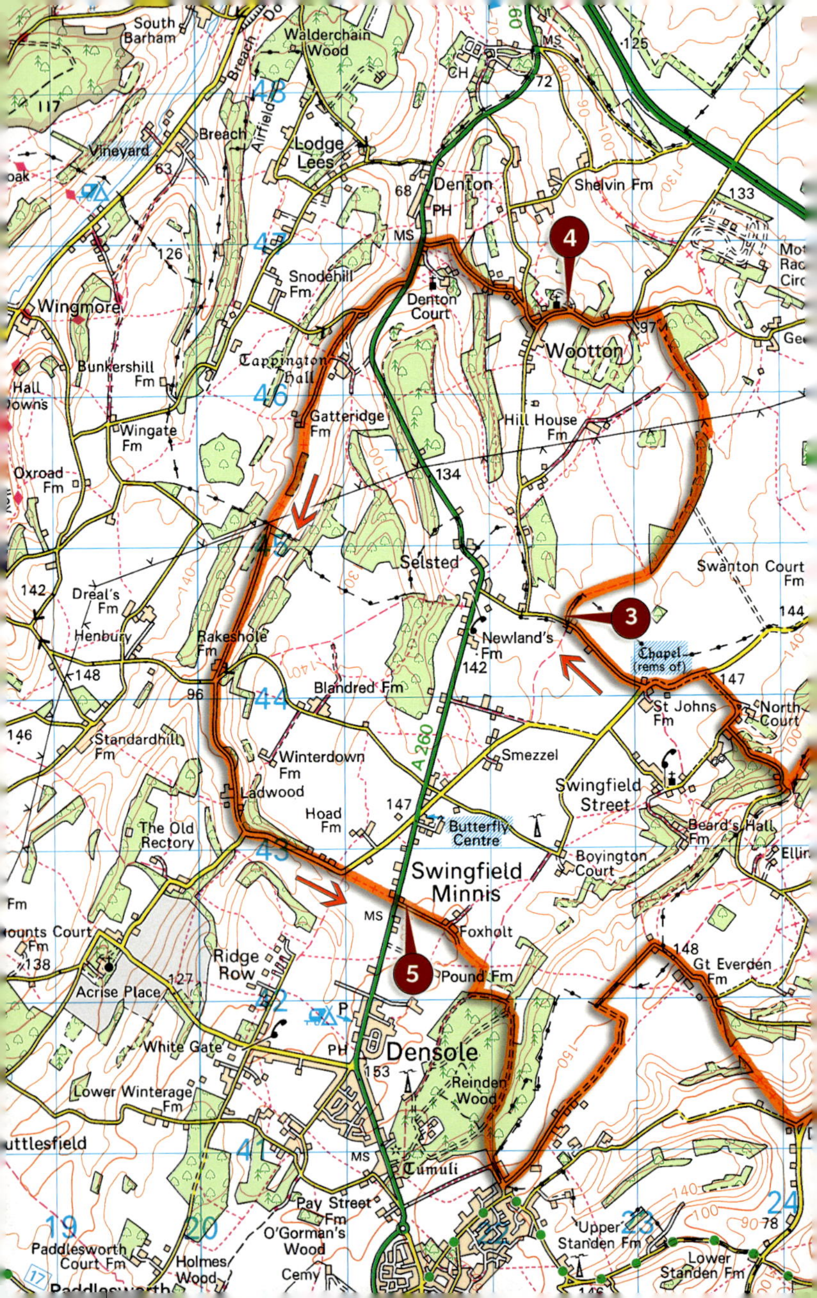
South Barham
Walderchain Wood
Breach
Airfield
Lodge Lees
Denton
PH
MS
CH
Shelvin Fm
Vineyard
Wingmore
Snodehill Fm
Denton Court
Wootton
4
Tappington Hall
Bunkershill Fm
Hall Downs
Gatteridge Fm
Hill House Fm
Wingate Fm
Oxroad Fm
Selsted
Swanton Court Fm
Dreal's Fm
Henbury
Rakeshole Fm
Newland's Fm
3
Chapel (rems of)
Blandred Fm
St Johns Fm
North Court
Standardhill Fm
Winterdown Fm
Smezzel
A 260
Swingfield Street
Ladwood
Hoad Fm
Butterfly Centre
Beard's Hall Fm
The Old Rectory
Boyington Court
Swingfield Minnis
Foxholt
Pound Fm
5
Gt Everden Fm
Ridge Row
Acrise Place
White Gate
Densole
Reinden Wood
Lower Winterage Fm
Tumuli
Pay Street Fm
O'Gorman's Wood
Upper Standen Fm
Lower Standen Fm
Paddlesworth Court Fm
Holmes Wood
Cemy

Alternative start/finish at Kearsney Abbey car park

(A) Turn → along the Alkham Road then take the **LH** turn by an imposing flint-built house (green byway signpost).

Pass a street sign (*Scotland Common*), then climb steeply and at length along the narrow tarmac lane; where the climb levels, tarmac gives way to a rutted (often muddy) earth track. Continue through woods then go through a stock gate to follow the track along the edge of woods fringing **The Minnis common**.

(2) At the far (**W**) end of the common, continue ↑ through a gate onto a restricted byway track that soon becomes tarmac road. Continue to a T-junction (*Lydden*) and turn → (↑). At a second T-junction, dogleg → then

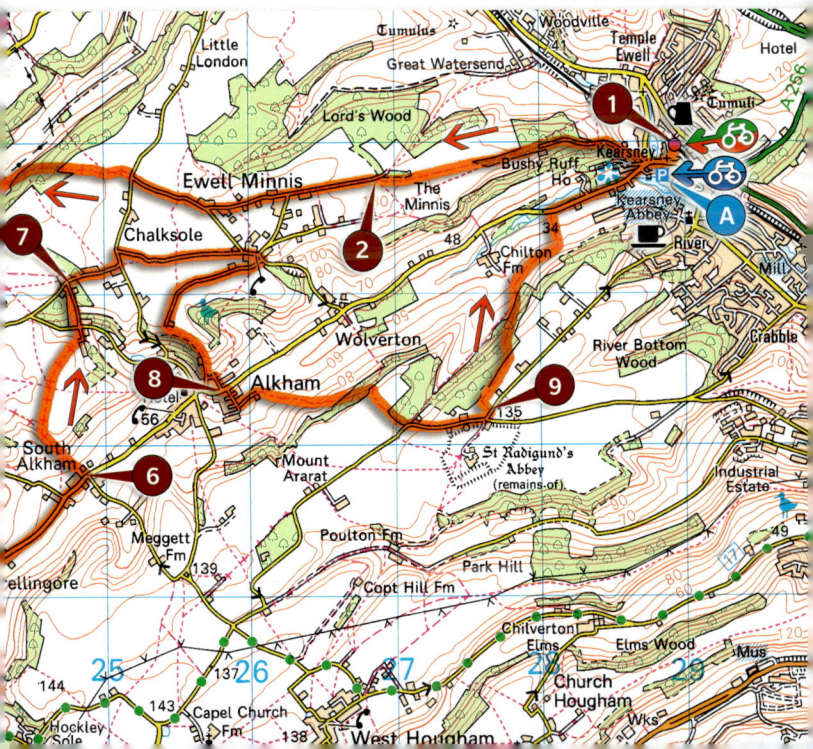

Heading east from Alkham

← onto a track (green byway sign). Cross open fields to a gate, go through and soon descend steeply on a sunken lane through Fidge's Wood. At the bottom of the descent, go through a stock gate and cross to the bottom edge of the field, bearing ← (SW) to continue on the byway. Go through a gate at the field edge and turn → onto a minor road at a bend. Climb steeply to a T-junction, turn → (*Lydden*) and follow the road around a sharp bend to another T-junction. Turn ← and after 500m, turn → along a narrow lane opposite **St John's Farm**.

3 After 750m, turn → onto a track road (green bridleway signpost); the surfaced track swings **right** near the entrance to a field and becomes an earth path, which can be very overgrown in summer. The path enters woodland – muddy in places – then climbs a little before emerging into a field. Continue ↑ across the field, then along the edge of woods to arrive at a minor road. Turn ← and soon climb steadily.

4 Arriving in **Wootton**, pass the **church**, turn → along Denton Lane (*Denton* and *Folkestone*), keeping ← at a fork before descending steeply to a T-junction. Turn ← onto the `A260` for 300m then turn → onto Snode Hill, soon turning ← onto a byway track (no sign) and continuing along the valley floor for 2.5km. The track passes **Rakeshole Farm** then arrives at a ✗ – continue ↑ along a narrow country lane. At a T-junction, turn ← (*Swingfield* and *Lydden*) and climb along the road, keeping ↑ onto a byway track where the road bends sharp left. At a ✗, cross ↑ over the `A260`.

5 From Fox Holt Road continue on the bridleway following the track around to a multiple path junction at the edge of **Reinden Wood**. Turn → (S) on the bridleway to the right of a metal stock gate. On entering the woods turn ← along the bridleway, keeping ← at a fork, then ↑ at a ✖ before bearing ← again at another fork to climb out of the wood and emerge onto a farm road. Bear ← (↑), pass Fernfield Farm and turn ← onto Fernfield Lane at a T-junction. Follow a narrow road between open fields then around right angles to **Great Everden Farm**. Pass by the farm and where the road bends sharp left, keep ↑ on a narrow lane, shortly turning → onto a byway track. The track soon begins descending very steeply along a sunken lane, which has a deep rut along the middle. The track spits you out on a narrow lane; turn ← then ← again onto the Alkham Road (*Alkham* and *Kearsney*) – **this is a fast road so ride with care**.

6 After 1km turn ← onto a byway track. The flinty track soon climbs very steeply; keep → at a fork near the top of the climb. Go through a gate and continue along a field edge on a rutted path that can be very muddy. Descend steeply to cross a minor road (Slip Lane – green byway sign) and immediately start climbing again on a steep-sided flinty track with the added challenge of a very deep rut along the middle. If you reach the top without a dab, you're doing well!

7 Arrive at a minor road, turn → to continue to a T-junction then dogleg ← then → and continue to **Ewell Minnis**. At a ✖ with a red telephone box, keep ↑ (→) then turn immediately → onto Green Lane – a restricted

Descending towards Kearsney

byte. Continue along the track, which eventually passes a house (watch out for goats and geese!), turns sharp **left** and becomes very narrow as it runs alongside a fence – this path can be very overgrown in summer. Pass through a gate and descend across an open hillside with fine views over Alkham. Make for a gate, go through and continue descending to a road.

8 Turn ← onto the busy Alkham Valley Road through **Alkham**, then → onto Short Lane after 150m. Descend along a residential road and turn ← at the bottom onto a (signposted) bridleway. Continue through a gate and begin climbing steeply along a field edge on the flank of a magnificent steep escarpment. Pass through a gateway, descend a little then climb very steeply to go through a gate into woodland. Keep → at a fork and follow the narrowing path between fields before descending to a minor road. Turn ← and climb a little then turn ← at a ✖ onto Minnis Lane (*River*).

9 Turn ← onto a (signposted) bridleway almost immediately, then bear → at a path ✖ to follow the narrow bridleway alongside a barbed wire fence. The bridleway soon bears **left** away from the fence and descends steeply through Gorsehill Wood on a rutted, flinty path. Go through a gate, descend a little further to go through another gate then turn sharp → through yet another gate to continue contouring along a paddock edge (there may be horses) on a vague bridleway path. Descend a little then go through a gate on your left next to a padlocked gate. Follow the field edge a short way, look out for a blue bridleway waymarker pointing left and descend across an arable field to arrive at a road. Turn → along the road to continue into **Kearsney**.

Autumnal woodland, St Martha's Hill

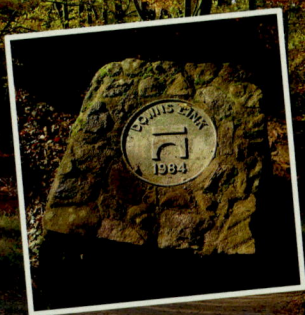

The Downs Link

START	Trailhead at St Martha's Hill **TQ 032 484**; or Guildford train station **SU 992 496**
FINISH	Shoreham-by-Sea train station **TQ 218 053**; or Brighton train station **TQ 310 049**
DISTANCE	59km (37 miles); or 77.5km (48¼ miles)
ON ROAD	4.75km (3 miles); or 14.5km (9 miles)
OFF ROAD	54.25km (34 miles); or 63km (39¼ miles)
ASCENT	465m (1525ft); or 705m (2315ft)
GRADE	▲
TIME	4hrs–4hrs 30mins; or 5hrs 30mins–6hrs
MAPS	OS Explorer 145, Landranger 186, 187, 198
PUB	Many en route, including The Partridge at Partridge Green
CAFÉ	Many en route, including Hatties Home Baked in Southwater

90%
OFF ROAD

At the start of the Downs Link long-distance path on St Martha's Hill

St Martha's Hill

Chinthurst Lane

Cranleigh/B2130

Baynards

Downs Link/Sussex Border Path

River Arun

Christ's Hospital

Southwater

Betley Bridge

Henfield, Upper Station Road

River Arun

King's Stone Avenue, Bramber

River Adur/ Coast Link Path

Shoreham-by-Sea

300

200

100

0   5   10   15   20   25   30   35   40   45   50   55   60km

Overview

The Downs Link long-distance path, which was established in 1984, begins at St Martha's Hill on the NDW and wends its sinuous way along wooded downland paths before dropping down to the Low Weald and following the course of dismantled railway lines southeast through Surrey and Sussex to cross the South Downs Way near Steyning. The first section provides the characteristic mix of off-road riding trails found across the North Downs while the route across the Weald on generally well-surfaced and largely level tree and shrub-lined tracks lets you build up a head of steam as you head towards the South Downs. However, the Downs Link is not to be underestimated – it is a long ride and the subtle gradients encountered here and there require some effort. Riding south into a southerly wind would also make for hard work. Although the route is extensively waymarked, it is still possible to go astray so do not let yourself be hypnotised into inattentiveness by the long, straight sections!

As this is a linear route, it makes sense to travel by train to the start and from the finish. St Martha's Hill is a 7km ride southwest from Guildford and adds some enjoyable broad sandy tracks to the start of the ride. At the southern end of the Downs Link a 5km extension known as the Coastal Link takes you along the River Adur to Shoreham-by-Sea, where there is also a train station. However, as long as you still have some energy, it is worth continuing for 7km east along the coast to Brighton. The prevailing south-westerlies mean that you are likely to have the wind at your back and you are also likely to arrive at Brighton mainline railway station faster than if you wait for a train at Shoreham-by-Sea!

The route passes through or near small towns and villages at regular intervals should you need refreshments. There are also several picnic stops en route including those at several of the former stations along the route. Also at regular intervals there are marker posts giving the distance to the next town or village on the route and the remaining distance to the South Downs Way. The Downs Link is also well-used by horse riders and dog walkers in particular – slow down and give way to other users.

Directions

Alternative start from Guildford station

(A) Follow the one-way system around to join the `A281` Shalford road. After 650m, join the cycle path running parallel to the right-hand side of the road; follow this for 600m before turning **←** (*NDW*) and crossing back over the `A281` onto a residential road (**PW**). Continue up the road for 400m before turning **→** onto a track road (*NDW*); follow the track round past a parking area as it climbs to the **left** of Chantry Cottage. Continue on this excellent track along the edge of the **Chantries woodland**. **Beware of an area of soft sand, which may stop you in your tracks.**

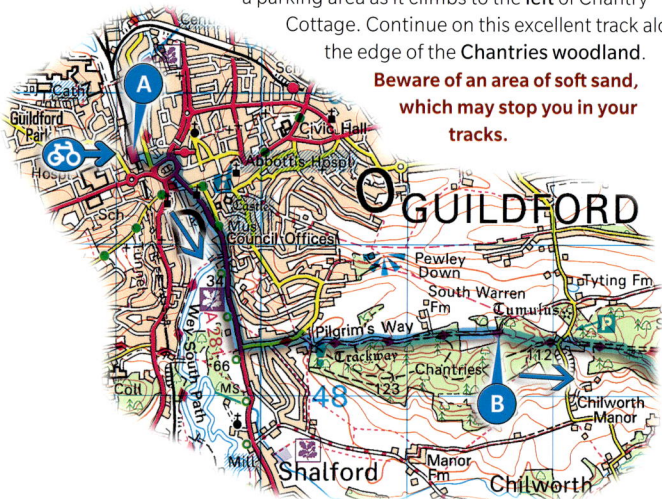

(B) At a ✖, continue **↑** through woodland. At a second ✖, keep **↑** and climb to a T-junction with a lane; dogleg **←** then **→** (*NDW*) and climb steeply up the flank of **St Martha's Hill** following *NDW* signs. At a fork, the good uphill track becomes footpath only, so turn **→** and contour around the hill on a frequently unridable soft sand track; this is one occasion when wet weather helps by firming the sand up. Once the track starts descending you may gain enough traction to stay upright. At a path T-junction, keep **↑** along the bridleway. At the next ✖, near a Second World War pill box, turn **→** where a signpost indicates the *Downs Link (DL) trail*.

1 From the trailhead at **St Martha's Hill**, pass the stone marker with brass plaque marking the start of the LDP and soon begin descending quite steeply; **exercise caution as the exciting descent features soft sand, bricks and tree roots**, which will put you on the deck if you do not have your wits about you. Having survived the main descent, continue downhill on a good track and

keep ← at a T-junction. At a ✖ with the `A248`, cross the road ↑ and continue along a lane and over a bridge. The DL soon forks **right** off the lane between a hedgerow and a fence; continue along the wooded bridleway (footpath parallel) which can get very churned up by horse hooves. On emerging from the woods, fork → and continue across Rosemary Hill and Blackheath on sandy paths through pine forest.

2 Cross ↑ over a minor road (Sampleoak Lane) and soon pass to the right of a large house. Keep ↑ (←) at a ✖ then descend quite steeply, passing through **Great Tangley Manor** before entering woodland. Shortly before the main bridleway emerges onto the `B2128`, turn → onto a narrow path (**the Downs Link signpost is easily missed**) and shortly arrive at a ✖ with the road shortly after. Cross ↑ over the road and continue along the track, turning → (*DL marker* on a post) at a ✖. Continue on a good path, turning ← at a T-junction then passing Chinthurst Farm before emerging at a ✖ on Chinthurst Lane.

3 Cross ↑ to join a minor road; the DL path keeps to the right of the road for a short stretch before arriving at a bridge; turn ← on the bridleway (*NCN22*) and almost immediately → to cross the lower bridge before turning ← along the canal. After 1km pass through the disused **Bramley and Wonersh station** and cross ↑ over the `B2128`. All you need do for the next 7km is keep the pedals

Old station sign, Bramley

turning as you head southeast on the well-surfaced, virtually level track that follows the course of a disused canal and a dismantled railway line. Arriving at the outskirts of **Cranleigh**, cross ↑ over the `B2130` and continue on the track, which skirts the edge of town with fields to the right. Cross ↑ over a minor road and continue past a leisure centre and playing fields. After a further 4.5km you will pass the restored **Baynards station** – the last train passed through in June 1965. Go through a gate then dogleg ← then → through another gate to continue along the bridleway track.

Downs Link signpost near Rudgwick

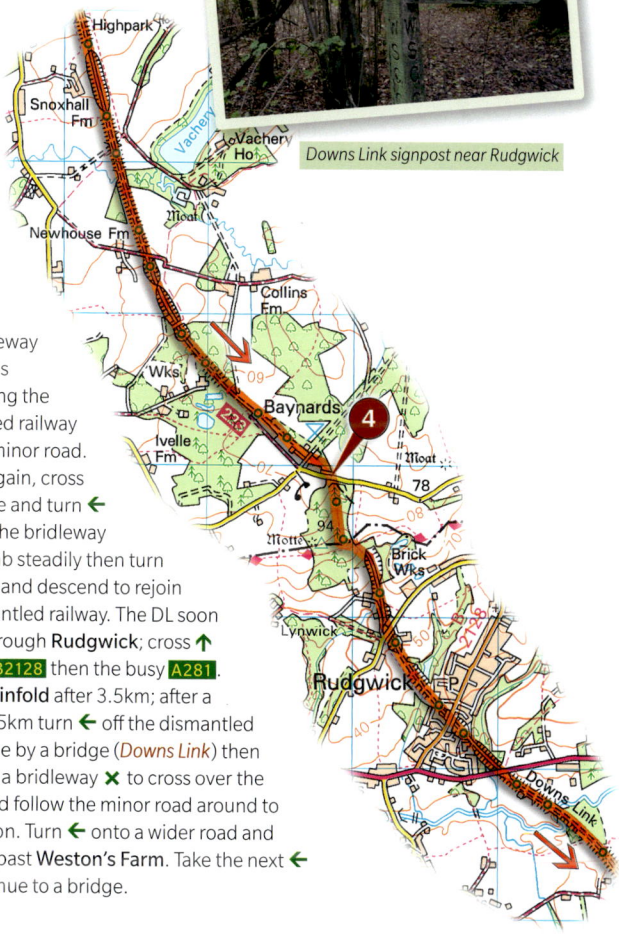

4 The bridleway soon turns **left**, leaving the dismantled railway to join a minor road. Turn ← again, cross the bridge and turn ← to rejoin the bridleway (*DL*). Climb steadily then turn ← at a ✗ and descend to rejoin the dismantled railway. The DL soon passes through **Rudgwick**; cross ↑ over the B2128 then the busy A281. Pass by **Slinfold** after 3.5km; after a further 2.5km turn ← off the dismantled railway line by a bridge (*Downs Link*) then turn → at a bridleway ✗ to cross over the bridge and follow the minor road around to a T-junction. Turn ← onto a wider road and continue past **Weston's Farm**. Take the next ← and continue to a bridge.

5 Cross the
bridge over
the railway
then turn ➜ by
the playing fields of
Christ's Hospital school.
Turn ➜ off the tarmac
road onto a bridleway track
soon passing through a fence
that sits on the **right** to continue on
the dismantled railway. Continue into
Southwater, passing under a bridge then
passing by the health centre to rejoin the

dismantled railway track. The DL soon passes under the `A24` and 3.75km further on you will arrive at the former West Grinstead station, now a picnic site and car park. Pass under a bridge beneath the `A272` and continue along the bridleway. After 3.5km the DL joins the `B2135` at **Partridge Green**. Stay with the road for 500m before turning ← onto a track road. At a ✖, turn → to rejoin the dismantled railway and soon go through a gate to cross a grassy field that can be very wet and muddy at times. Go through another gate, cross a bridge over the River Adur and continue for a further 1.5km.

6 Reaching Upper Station Road at the west end of **Henfield**, dogleg ← then → to continue down Station Road, passing a cul-de-sac wittily named Beechings. At a T-junction at the bottom of the road, dogleg → then ← to rejoin the DL on the dismantled railway. After 3km the DL crosses another bridge over the River Adur then shortly after it leaves the dismantled railway behind and heads across country, climbing a little on a good track. The bridleway turns sharp **left** and descends through **Wyckham Farm** where it becomes a good gravel track. The track gives way to tarmac along King's Barn Lane.

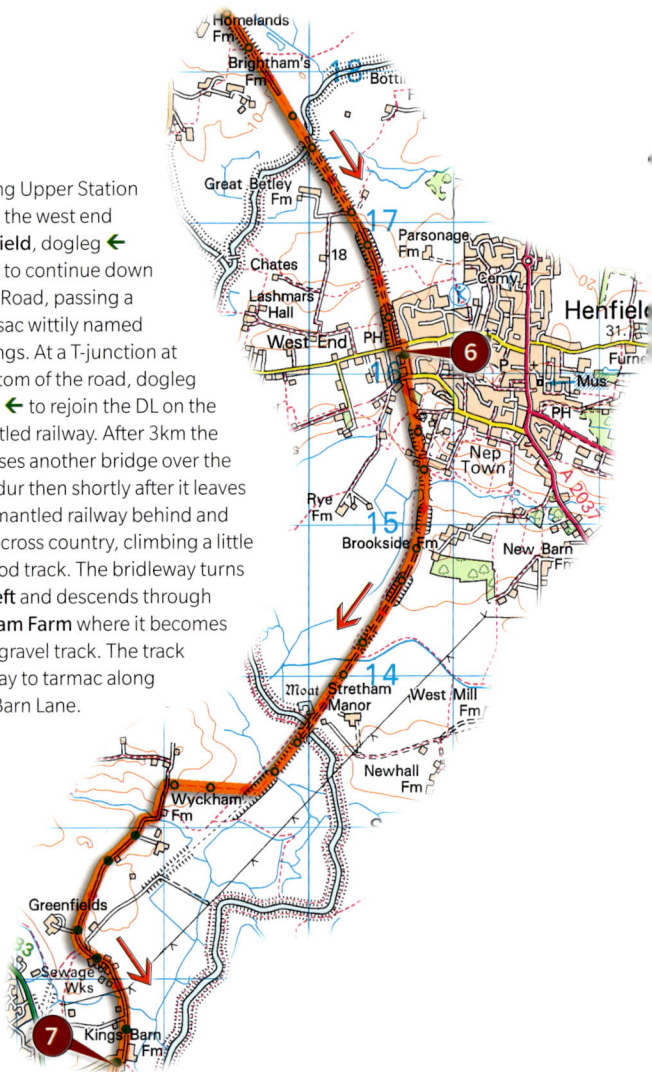

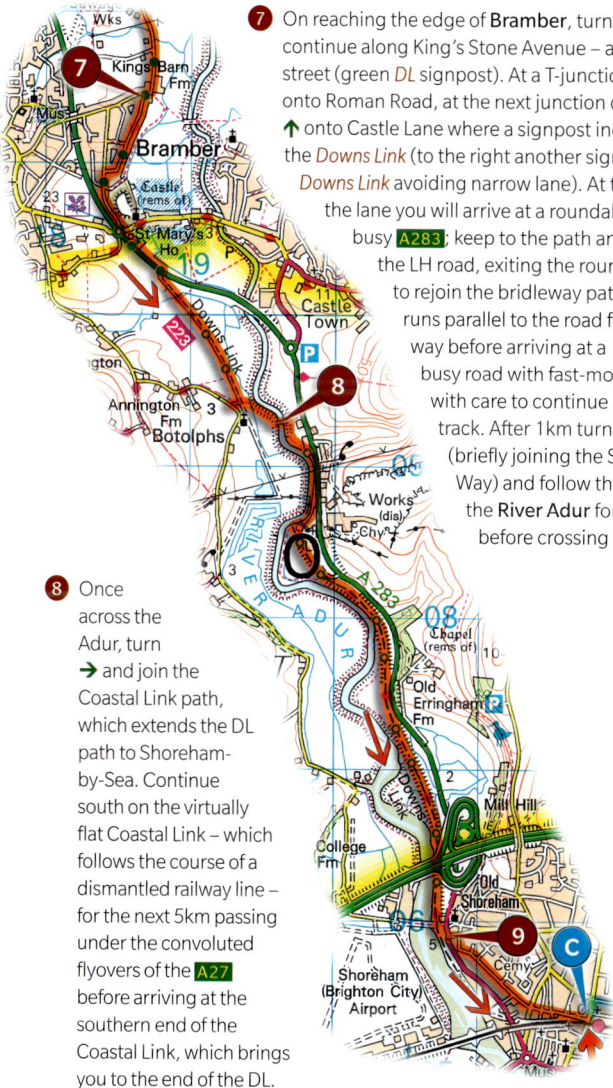

7 On reaching the edge of **Bramber**, turn → then ← to continue along King's Stone Avenue – a residential street (green *DL* signpost). At a T-junction, turn ← onto Roman Road, at the next junction continue ↑ onto Castle Lane where a signpost indicates the *Downs Link* (to the right another sign indicates *Downs Link* avoiding narrow lane). At the end of the lane you will arrive at a roundabout on the busy `A283`; keep to the path and cross over the LH road, exiting the roundabout ↑ to rejoin the bridleway path. The path runs parallel to the road for a short way before arriving at a ✗ – cross the busy road with fast-moving traffic with care to continue along a good track. After 1km turn ← at a ✗ (briefly joining the South Downs Way) and follow the bank of the **River Adur** for a short way before crossing a bridge.

8 Once across the Adur, turn → and join the Coastal Link path, which extends the DL path to Shoreham-by-Sea. Continue south on the virtually flat Coastal Link – which follows the course of a dismantled railway line – for the next 5km passing under the convoluted flyovers of the `A27` before arriving at the southern end of the Coastal Link, which brings you to the end of the DL.

9 Just past a large old footbridge over the **River Arun**, turn ➔ onto the `A283` to continue into **Shoreham-by-Sea**. For the station turn ⬅ then ➔ off the roundabout onto Upper Shoreham Road, and turn ➔ along Connaught Avenue, arriving at **Shoreham-by-Sea station** after 1.25km.

Alternative finish at Brighton station

C From **Shoreham-by-Sea station**, turn ⬅ (*NCN2*) along Buckingham Road, then take the second ➔ (Rosslyn Road) and fol-low *NCN2* signs through **Shoreham** and **Shoreham Harbour**, then back along the coast along the `A259` into Brighton. After passing the ruins of the West Pier on your right and Brighton Centre on your left, turn ⬅ onto the `A2010`, soon arriving at **Brighton station**.

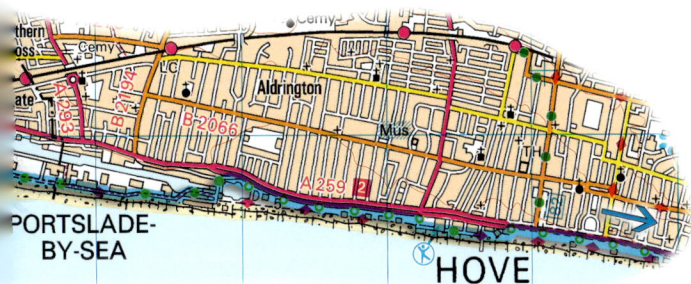

Appendix A
Camping and accommodation

Wild camping

Much of the North Downs is managed woodland and cultivated land, so wild camping can be problematic. Legally you are not allowed to wild camp on any land without permission, however publicans and farmers may allow you to camp on their land if you ask their permission first; having done so you should be discreet, avoid crops and leave no litter; please do NOT light any fires.

Campsites

There is hardly an abundance of campsites around the North Downs; some YHA hostels permit camping in their grounds, see the YHA website for details: www.yha.org.uk.

Dunn Street Farm
(camping and caravan site)
Westwell, Ashford TN25 4NJ
Tel: 01233 71253

Bush Road
Cuxton, Rochester
Kent ME2 1HF
Tel: 01634 296829

Woolmans Wood
Rochester Road, Rochester
Medway ME5 9SB
Tel: 01634 867685
woolmans.wood@currantbun.com

Gate House Wood Touring Park
(camping and caravan site)
Ford Lane, Wrotham Heath
Kent TN15 7SD
Tel: 01732 843062

Hostels and Camping Barns

YHA Puttenham Camping Barn
The Street, Puttenham,
Near Guildford
Surrey GU3 1AR
Tel: 0800 0191700 (bookings);
01483 811001 (arrivals)
campingbarns@yha.org.uk

YHA Holmbury
Radnor Lane, Dorking
Surrey RH5 6NW
Tel: 0845 371 932
holmbury@yha.org.uk

YHA Tanner's Hatch,
off Ranmore Common Road
Dorking
Surrey RH5 6BE
Tel: 0845 371 9542
tanners@yha.org.uk

YHA Hindhead
Devil's Punchbowl, off Portsmouth Road
Thursley, Godalming
Surrey GU8 6NS
Tel: 0845 371 9022
hindhead@yha.org.uk

YHA Cold Blow Farm Camping Barn
Cold Blow Lane, Thurnham
Kent ME14 3LR
Tel: 0800 0191700 (bookings);
01622 730439 (arrivals)
campingbarns@yha.org.uk

YHA Canterbury
54 New Dover Road
Canterbury CT1 3DT
Tel: 0845 371 9010
canterbury@yha.org.uk

North Downs Barn
Bush Road
Cuxton, Rochester
Kent ME2 1HF
Tel: 01634 296829

Appendix B

Bike shops/bike hire/ bike mechanics

Head for the Hills
43–44 West Street
Dorking
Surrey RH4 1BU
Tel: 01306 885007
www.head-for-the-hills.co.uk

Nirvana Cycles
5 The Green
Guildford Road
Westcott, Dorking
Surrey RH4 3NR
Tel: 01306 740300
www.nirvanacycles.com

Cycleworks
218 London Road
Burpham, Guildford
Surrey GU4 7JS
Tel: 01483 302210
guildford@cycleworks.co.uk
www.cycleworks.co.uk/guildford

Pedal Pushers
75 Stoke Road
Guildford
Surrey GU1 4HT
Tel: 01483 502 327
www.pedalpushers.co

Pedal and Spoke
The Little Shop
Walking Bottom
Peaslake
Surrey GU5 9RR
Tel: 01306 73163
www.pedalandspoke.co.uk

Cycleworks
19–21 West Street
Haslemere
Surrey GU27 2AB
Tel: 01428 648424
haslemere@cycleworks.co.uk
www.cycleworks.co.uk/haslemere

WyndyMilla Ltd
Manor Farm Cycle Centre
Wood Lane
Seale
Surrey GU10 1HR
Tel: 01252 782960
themob@wyndymilla.com
www.wyndymilla.com

Finch Cycles
43 Bell Street
Reigate
Surrey RH2 7AQ
Tel: 01737 242163
www.finchcycles.co.uk

Petra Cycles
90 Station Road East
Oxted
Surrey RH8 0QA
Tel: 01883 715114
www.petracycles.co.uk

C & N Cycles
32 Station Road
Redhill
Surrey RH1 1PD
Tel: 01737 760857
www.candncycles.co.uk

Surrey Hills Mountain Bike Guides
offer a pick-up and drop-off or delivery
and collection bike hire service, visit:
www.surreyhillsmountainbikeguides.co.uk.

Appendix C
Useful contacts

Public transport and accommodation

For train timetable information and to book
tickets online: www.nationalrail.co.uk. For
National Rail enquiries, tel: 08457 484 950.

North Downs area mountain biking clubs, associations and websites

Surrey

www.mtbsurreyhills.com

www.muddymoles.org.uk

www.surreyhillsmtber.co.uk

Kent

www.kent-trails.co.uk

www.porc.uk.com
(Penshurst Off Road Cycling)

www.mountainbikinginkent.co.uk

www.mccoffroad.co.uk

Notes

Listing of Cicerone Guides

Rocky Rambler's Wild Walks
Scrambles in the Lake District
　North & South
Short Walks in Lakeland
　1 South Lakeland
　2 North Lakeland
　3 West Lakeland
The Cumbria Coastal Way
The Cumbria Way and the
　Allerdale Ramble
Tour of the Lake District

DERBYSHIRE, PEAK DISTRICT AND MIDLANDS

High Peak Walks
Scrambles in the Dark Peak
The Star Family Walks
Walking in Derbyshire
White Peak Walks
　The Northern Dales
　The Southern Dales

SOUTHERN ENGLAND

Suffolk Coast & Heaths Walks
The Cotswold Way
The North Downs Way
The Peddars Way and Norfolk
　Coast Path
The Ridgeway National Trail
The South Downs Way
The South West Coast Path
The Thames Path
Walking in Berkshire
Walking in Essex
Walking in Kent
Walking in Norfolk
Walking in Sussex
Walking in the Cotswolds
Walking in the Isles of Scilly
Walking in the New Forest
Walking in the Thames Valley
Walking on Dartmoor
Walking on Guernsey
Walking on Jersey
Walking on the Isle of Wight
Walks in the South Downs
　National Park

WALES AND WELSH BORDERS

Backpacker's Britain – Wales
Glyndwr's Way
Great Mountain Days
　in Snowdonia
Hillwalking in Snowdonia

Hillwalking in Wales: 1&2
Offa's Dyke Path
Ridges of Snowdonia
Scrambles in Snowdonia
The Ascent of Snowdon
The Ceredigion and Snowdonia
　Coast Paths
Lleyn Peninsula Coastal Path
Pembrokeshire Coastal Path
The Severn Way
The Shropshire Hills
The Wye Valley Walk
Walking in Pembrokeshire
Walking in the Forest of Dean
Walking in the South
　Wales Valleys
Walking on Gower
Walking on the Brecon Beacons
Welsh Winter Climbs

INTERNATIONAL CHALLENGES, COLLECTIONS AND ACTIVITIES

Canyoning
Europe's High Points
The Via Francigena
　(Canterbury to Rome): 1&2

EUROPEAN CYCLING

Cycle Touring in France
Cycle Touring in Ireland
Cycle Touring in Spain
Cycle Touring in Switzerland
Cycling in the French Alps
Cycling the Canal du Midi
Cycling the River Loire
The Danube Cycleway
The Grand Traverse of the
　Massif Central
The Rhine Cycle Route
The Way of St James

AFRICA

Climbing in the Moroccan
　Anti-Atlas
Kilimanjaro
Mountaineering in the Moroccan
　High Atlas
The High Atlas
Trekking in the Atlas Mountains
Walking in the Drakensberg

ALPS – CROSS-BORDER ROUTES

100 Hut Walks in the Alps
Across the Eastern Alps: E5
Alpine Points of View

Alpine Ski Mountaineering
　1 Western Alps
　2 Central and Eastern Alps
Chamonix to Zermatt
Snowshoeing
Tour of Mont Blanc
Tour of Monte Rosa
Tour of the Matterhorn
Trekking in the Alps
Trekking in the Silvretta and
　Rätikon Alps
Walking in the Alps
Walks and Treks in the
　Maritime Alps

PYRENEES AND FRANCE/SPAIN CROSS-BORDER ROUTES

Rock Climbs in the Pyrenees
The GR10 Trail
The Mountains of Andorra
The Pyrenean Haute Route
The Pyrenees
The Way of St James
Through the Spanish Pyrenees:
　GR11
Walks and Climbs in the Pyrenees

AUSTRIA

The Adlerweg
Trekking in Austria's Hohe Tauern
Trekking in the Stubai Alps
Trekking in the Zillertal Alps
Walking in Austria

EASTERN EUROPE

The High Tatras
The Mountains of Romania
Walking in Bulgaria's
　National Parks
Walking in Hungary

FRANCE

Chamonix Mountain Adventures
Ecrins National Park
GR20: Corsica
Mont Blanc Walks
Mountain Adventures in
　the Maurienne
The Cathar Way
The GR5 Trail
The Robert Louis Stevenson Trail
Tour of the Oisans: The GR54
Tour of the Queyras
Tour of the Vanoise
Trekking in the Vosges and Jura

Walking – Trekking – Mountaineering – Climbing – Cycling

Over 40 years, Cicerone have built up an outstanding collection of 300 guides, inspiring all sorts of amazing adventures.

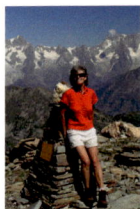

Every guide comes from extensive exploration and research by our expert authors, all with a passion for their subjects. They are frequently praised, endorsed and used by clubs, instructors and outdoor organisations.

All our titles can now be bought as **e-books** and many as iPad and Kindle files and we will continue to make all our guides available for these and many other devices.

Our website shows any **new information** we've received since a book was published. Please do let us know if you find anything has changed, so that we can pass on the latest details. On our **website** you'll also find some great ideas and lots of information, including sample chapters, contents lists, reviews, articles and a photo gallery.

It's easy to keep in touch with what's going on at Cicerone, by getting our monthly **free e-newsletter**, which is full of offers, competitions, up-to-date information and topical articles. You can subscribe on our home page and also follow us on **Facebook** and **Twitter**, as well as our **blog**.

Cicerone – the very best guides for exploring the world.

CICERONE

2 Police Square Milnthorpe Cumbria LA7 7PY
Tel: 015395 62069 info@cicerone.co.uk
www.cicerone.co.uk